The Theology of the Christian Year:
The Sermons of Father Robert Crouse

THE SOUL'S PILGRIMAGE

'Drawing on a deep knowledge of the Christian theological tradition these sermons by Father Crouse have a beautiful directness that illumines the eschatological character of the Christian year. Crouse's sermons are filled with insights that reflect the no doubt hard won wisdom of this remarkable human being and priest. For example, according to Crouse salvation is a kind of seeing acquired through attending to the words we are given in liturgy and prayer. The task of the preacher is to help us discover what time we are in by helping us see what God has done on the cross. Drawing on a wide range of literature Crouse's sermons make clear that the sermon is, can, and should be the genre for the work of theology.'

Stanley Hauerwas
Gilbert T. Rowe Professor Emeritus of Divinity and Law, Duke Divinity School, Duke University

'The opportunity to take an overview of the work of the shy Canadian scholar-pastor Robert Crouse is one that no one who has looked for hidden treasure will want to pass by. Here we meet him as a preacher, now set loose from the narrative of the seasons from Advent to Pentecost but still strictly faithful to the prescribed Scripture readings, ranging widely over the experience of the Christian life in general and especially in the University. We may be surprised first of all by the unpretentiousness of these homilies; but then we will be struck by the great care with which they have been composed to take their place within the act of worship, and by the intellectual discipline with which the Scripture text is called on to shed light on the tasks of faithful living. And finally, perhaps, we may be convinced that they form a whole greater than the sum of the parts, a structure of Christian living and worship, built in the pattern of the Anglican Prayer Book, that is both coherent and expansive.'

Oliver O'Donovan
Professor Emeritus, Christian Ethics and Practical Theology, School of Divinity, University of Edinburgh

'This second volume of homilies by Robert Crouse are a splendid complement to the first: each reflection on the Scriptures appointed for the seasons of Trinity and Pentecost is rich in lucid theological substance; in them the revealed Word itself shines forth in beauty and power. In the cycle of the year which recollects the testimony of saints down through centuries we are given further memorable demonstrations that, in the author's words, "the Church can have its true existence only in obedience to the Word of God made manifest in Jesus Christ." For Christians who may have only a modest acquaintance with their legacy in the 'cloud of witnesses' whose Christ-like examples urge us on, these homilies are a treasure trove of inspiration and illumination, a marvelous short course opening vistas on the Body of Christ against and across the ages, persevering in faithfulness unto the end.'

David Lyle Jeffrey
Emeritus Distinguished Professor of Literature and the Humanities, Baylor University

The Theology of the Christian Year:
The Sermons of Father Robert Crouse

THE SOUL'S PILGRIMAGE

Volume II: The Descent of the Dove and the Spiritual Life

R. D. CROUSE

Volume editors: Susan Dodd and Gary Thorne

Series editors: Stephen Blackwood, Neil Robertson and Gary Thorne

DARTON·LONGMAN+TODD

This collection published in 2024 by
Darton, Longman and Todd Ltd
1 Spencer Court
140 – 142 Wandsworth High Street
London SW18 4JJ

ISBN: 978-1-915412-64-5

A catalogue record for this book is available from the British Library.

Produced and designed by Judy Linard
Printed and bound by Replika Press Pvt Ltd, India

In Memoriam
Robert Darwin Crouse

Et erit ibi semita et via, et via sancta vocabitur.
Isaiah 35:8

Anon., *Cosmic Christ* tympanum, stone sculpture, c. 1130,
SSainte-Marie-Madeleine de Vézelay, Burgundy, France.

CONTENTS

Be not conformed to this world: but be ye
transformed by the renewing of your mind,
that ye may prove what is that good,
and acceptable, and perfect, will of God.
Romans 12:2

ACKNOWLEDGEMENTS

In addition to those listed in the first volume of sermons, we gratefully acknowledge the contributions of Rhea Bright, Clinton Collister, Jan Connors, Beth Eayrs, Jonathan Eayrs, Victoria Goddard, Paige Hochschild, Kara Holm, Fr Chris McCann, Fr Edward Rix, Andrew Thorne, Sandra Thorne, Marcus Tomalin and Karen Westhaver. Peter Bullerwell, Stuart Kinney, Peter O'Brien, Patricia Robertson, Henry Roper, and Erin Wagner generously helped to prepare the final text of this volume for publication.

THE WORKS OF ROBERT CROUSE

Robert Crouse (1930-2011) was a prominent Canadian theologian and scholar. He was a teacher, musician, preacher, and authority on Augustine and Dante. His interdisciplinary approach to scholarship, linking the arts, poetry, architecture, science, philosophy, music and theology of every age, influenced the way of thinking of thousands of students. As a preacher, his gift of intellect was filtered through a deeply pastoral spirit such that his sermons were received enthusiastically by world-class academics, keen university students, struggling parents, fishers, and farmers alike.

Pilgrimage, Human and Divine: The Works of Robert Crouse is a project to make available Crouse's writings that were previously unpublished or not widely available. The first volume in this series is *Images of Pilgrimage: Paradise and Wilderness in Christian Spirituality*, published in 2023. Next is the first volume of a three-volume collection of his sermons; the present volume is the second in that set. A third volume of sermons will complete the collection as Crouse describes the heavenly pilgrimage that is prior to all earthly pilgrimage: the pilgrimage within the life of God the Trinity as revealed in Holy Scripture.

Forthcoming also is *A Theology of Pilgrimage*, a collection of theological essays drawing on the Christian tradition to address contemporary issues. Finally, there are projected books on *Dante's Pilgrimage* – revealing Fr Crouse's spiritual vision in his teaching on *The Divine Comedy* – and a volume on Boethius.

Accessible, scholarly, pastoral, tightly argued, philosophically astute, and beautifully written, Crouse's writings speak profoundly to the tensions – sacred and profane – that are inherent in our divided and distracted culture. They point us to the supernatural hope that alone can bring reconciling justice to the earthly paradise in anticipation of the heavenly.

PREFACE

The late Reverend Canon Professor Robert Crouse continues to offer an authoritative voice within the Anglican Church of Canada and cast a critical vision in the global Church. This volume of his sermons, collected by the Revd Dr Gary Thorne and edited with Dr Susan Dodd, shows how Fr Crouse's commitment to the Anglican *Book of Common Prayer* and the Church year shaped his own Christian discipleship and was central to his influence in the lives of generations of students and clergy in the Anglican communion. Fr Crouse was a member of the Primate's Theological Commission of the Anglican Church in Canada in the late 1990s and early 2000s. His gracious presence, questions and comments at our meetings helped guide our work. Fr Crouse was a Renaissance man whose broad knowledge over many academic disciplines was extraordinary. Consequently, his students and those who heard him preach were regularly challenged to think more deeply and critically about the twentieth and twenty-first century Church. As such, he functioned as both an anchor and a lighthouse for the Body of Christ.

One aspect of Fr Crouse's theological contribution was his ability to be locally rooted in rural Nova Scotia while holding a broad vision of the Church across the centuries and continents. Key to this balance of the local and global was his commitment to the notion of being friends with God. This comes through time and again in this collection of sermons.

It is my great pleasure to highly recommend this volume of sermons to those who seek to critically engage the gospel and Christ's call in the present confusing and confused culture.

+Victoria Matthews

While serving as Suffragan Bishop of Toronto and Bishop of Edmonton, the Rt Revd Victoria Matthews chaired the Anglican Church of Canada's Primate's Theological Commission 1996-2007. From 2008 until her retirement in 2018 she served as Bishop of Christchurch in the Anglican Church in Aotearoa, New Zealand and Polynesia.

PILGRIMAGE: THE CHRISTIAN YEAR

Exploding Star

Christ-child teaching

The Scream

Christmas **Pre-Lent**

Advent (December) **Epiphany** **Lent**

Nativity icon

Sower of the Word

Cosmic Shepherd

Easter — Ascension — St John the Baptist — Trinity/Pentecost . . . November

Whitsunday

'Noli me tangere.'

Preaching to the birds

Vision of Paradise

INTRODUCTION: VOLUME II

A revealed pilgrimage for the human soul.

For Christians of all denominations this second volume of sermons of Robert Crouse provides practical signposts for the soul's sure pilgrimage into sanctification (holiness of life) amid the spiritual confusions of the twenty-first century.

For Robert Crouse, pilgrimage is the fundamental biblical theme of the spiritual life, beginning with the scriptural revelation of pilgrimage in the life of God the Holy Trinity. The Father knows Himself in His Word and the Holy Spirit binds the Father and Son together in mutual love. The Christian revelation of this primary eternal pilgrimage within the divine life of the Trinity will be the subject of a third volume of sermons, forthcoming. But in this second volume, this eternal pilgrimage manifests itself in the created order as the Father goes outside of Himself in His own creation in order to return the cosmos to Himself through the redeeming activity of His Son. This is the remarkable teaching of Scripture, and the experience of the early Christians.

Indeed, since the early centuries of the Church, this redeeming pilgrimage of God in which he enters his creation to draw it back into himself has been outlined and rehearsed in the two major cycles of the Christian Year, the Temporale and Sanctorale. Our illustrated timeline shows how the Temporale organizes the feasts centred on Christ according to the variable date of Easter and the fixed date of Christmas. The Sanctorale is the cycle of the fixed dates of the feasts of the saints. These two cycles run concurrent, intersect, and interpret each other throughout the moments of the Christian Year.

The Temporale consists of two almost equal halves. The first half begins by introducing us to the cosmic dimensions of the Christian faith in the season of Advent, preparing us to understand the universal significance of the Divine Son taking mortal flesh in the womb of the Virgin Mary. The Temporale then rehearses in turn the doctrines of Christ as revealed in his nativity, teaching, healing, temptations, passion, crucifixion, and resurrection. The Son completes his redeeming pilgrimage by returning home to the Father in his Ascension. Only with the return of the Son to his Father's right hand does the Holy Spirit descend upon the infant Church, to lead it into all Truth.

The Sundays that occupy the second half of the Temporale, from the Feast of Pentecost to the Sunday just prior to the next Advent Season, vary in number according to the date of Easter in a given year. This second half of the Temporale has a different character from what has come before, and the logic behind the movement from Sunday to Sunday is not as evident as in the first half that follows the life of Christ. Nonetheless, the general intent and character of Trinity/Pentecost Season (the second half of the Temporale) is explored by Fr Crouse in the opening sermons of this volume. The second half of the Temporale is dependent upon the first half: we first learn of the unimaginable love of God for us, and then we pour ourselves out in love to others with that same sacrificial love of Christ. Having learned Christ in the first half of the Temporale, in Trinity/Pentecost Season we are taught how to allow Christ to live in and through us. What Christ has done *for* us, he must do *in* us, as we become more and more Christ-like.

The Spirit is sent to be born in us so that the life of Christ might be manifest in us. 'I am crucified with Christ: nevertheless I live; yet not I, but Christ liveth in me' (Gal. 2:20). The preaching of the Sanctorale, the commemoration of the saints, belongs to this volume II because the saints show what God in Christ does *in* us by the power of the Holy Spirit. The lives of the saints give witness precisely to this power of the Holy Spirit to transform our lives in holiness. Finally, the Holy Spirit has poured himself out on all flesh. The Holy Spirit is active not only in the life-changing and continuing conversion of baptised individuals, but also in the sanctification of our churches and human institutions. And so the final few sermons in this volume reflect upon the theme of pilgrimage in the ordered life of the Church and in the secular university.

In fact, all of reality is nothing but the desire for its conversion or spiritual pilgrimage to its home in the Father through Jesus Christ, by the power of the Holy Spirit. The whole of creation groans in longing for its return to its Creator (Romans 8:22), and Fr Crouse reminds us that humankind is nature's priest in bringing the created order to its final redemption. Scripture tells us that we are a 'kind of first fruits' of the redemption of the entire cosmos (James 1:18). The biblical account of the Christian soul's pilgrimage to its redemption in Christ by the power of the Holy Spirit inspired the early Church in its shaping of the Christian Year. By following the spiritual path of the Temporale and the witness of the Sanctorale we too participate in the redemption of the cosmos.

Our preacher often points out how the biblical theme of pilgrimage in the Christian Year governed the mind of the entire Western Church, influencing the art, architecture, and culture of Christendom through the ages. He cites as one example our frontispiece, the carved tympanum above the western portal of the nave of the twelfth-century basilica, Sainte-Marie-Madeleine, at Vézelay, in Burgundy. Not only itself the destination of pilgrims, the basilica was also the assembly point of pilgrims destined for St James Compostela. In *Images of Pilgrimage*, Fr Crouse describes how the basilica building intentionally illustrates the inner pilgrimage of the Christian mind and heart in the journey from darkness into light. He writes of the tympanum:

> The central figure is the cosmic Christ, surrounded by foliage and water, flanked by twelve apostles and St Paul, upon whom the Holy Spirit's rays descend from the outstretched hands of Christ, commissioning them to go forth into all the world. A border shows all the varied peoples of the earth; and outside that, another border shows the signs of the zodiac, with all the varied forms of human labour.
>
> Below that announcement of the meaning of the place, there is the figure of St John the Baptist, indicating the path of entrance. With astonishing architectural skill, the building is so oriented in its construction, that on St John the Baptist's Day the light from the clerestory windows makes a path of blocks of light precisely in the centre of the central aisle, from the dark narthex, right up the long and rather dimly lighted nave, straight to the altar, bathed in brilliant light. The pilgrim moves from darkness into light, from wilderness into paradise. The very structure of the building is an outward sign of the inner pilgrimage of spirit.

As Abbot Suger put it, speaking of the dedication of the Abbey Church of Saint-Denis in Paris, in 1140, 'That which is signified pleases more than that which signifies.' Inscribed upon the golden doors of Saint-Denis were the lines:

> Bright is the noble work; but being nobly bright, the work
> Should brighten the minds, so that they may
> travel through the true lights
> To the True Light where Christ is the True Door.

The Christian pilgrim in the twenty-first century journeys the same path of redemption in Jesus Christ as Christians have done in every age. Whether or not you worship in a liturgical church that follows the Christian Year, and regardless of the lectionary your denomination may follow, your spiritual vision and appreciation of the Spirit's presence in the Church will be enriched by these sermons. We are all part of that one communion of saints who, by God's grace, will one day 'fall down before him that sat on the throne, and worship him that liveth for ever and ever, and cast their crowns before the throne, saying, "Thou art worthy, O Lord, to receive glory and honour and power: for thou hast created all things, and for thy pleasure they are and were created"' (Revelation 4:10-11).

In this volume of sermons we are reminded that the wondrous diversity of saints with their many different gifts, struggles and callings are all expressions of one faith, one hope, and one all-embracing charity that builds the body in love.

May these sermons of Robert Crouse serve for you as signposts along the way of that grace-filled Christian pilgrimage of the Christian Year, taking you *further up and further into* the pilgrimage of the Son of God Himself. His pilgrimage began as

He left His Father's side to journey to find us in our wanderings. He comes to where we are, places us on His shoulders and continues His pilgrimage back to His Father and our Father. Thus our pilgrimage is nothing other than that of the Lord Jesus Christ Himself *in* us. He is our sanctification. He has come to take us home. He invites us to step onto the pilgrim road with Him. He, who is the same yesterday, and today, and forever (Hebrews 13:8) is our way, our pilgrimage home.

Gary Thorne

Feast of O Sapientia, 2023

Notes for the sermons are presented at the back of the book. These indicate the Scriptures accompanying the sermons and references to other works that Fr Crouse quotes. We have presented the sermons in the main text without footnotes or citations, so that the reader may encounter them as closely as possible to how they were received when preached. The texts that we share here are simply the notes from which Father Crouse preached.

INTRODUCTION TO TRINITY/ PENTECOST SEASON

TRINITY 1/ PENTECOST 2

Beloved, if God so loved us, we ought also to love one another.

The Church's year is divided into two parts, of roughly equal duration. The first part, approximately twenty-five weeks, runs from Advent to Trinity Sunday, and during those weeks, the Church sets before us in succession those mighty acts of God whereby our redemption is accomplished. The coming of the son of God to take upon him our flesh, the manifestation of his glory in the human life of Jesus, his suffering and death, his resurrection and ascension and the gift of the Spirit. All of this is summed up in our adoration of God, Father, Son and Spirit, on the Festival of the Holy Trinity.

Now on this first Sunday after Trinity, we enter upon the second half of the Church year; and the scriptures for today recapitulate what has gone before, and set the theme for the whole of the long Trinity season, and the theme is this:

'Beloved, if God so loved us, we ought also to love one another.'

The whole succession of these acts of God which we have celebrated are to be seen as a manifestation of the love of God.

> O love how deep, how broad, how high
> It fills the soul with ecstasy

That God, the son of God should take
Our mortal form for mortals' sake.

In this was manifest the love of God towards us, because that God sent his only begotten Son into the world, that we might live through him. We have seen and do testify that the Father sent the Son to be the saviour of the world. Herein is love: not that we loved God, but that he loved us, and sent his Son to be the propitiation for our sins.

'Beloved, if God so loved us, we ought also to love one another.'

For half the year then, we have celebrated the manifestation of God's love; and now, as we enter upon the second half of the year – the Trinity season – we draw a certain conclusion from all this:

'Beloved, if God so loved us, we ought also to love one another.'

The scriptures appointed for today and for the following Sundays after Trinity are selected precisely to instruct us in the nature of the divine love and how that love is to be acted out in human life. We ought also to love one another.

The prescription is simple enough, to be sure. Love God and love your neighbour. That is the fulfilling of the law. There is no greater commandment.

It appears simple enough: supremely simple. And yet, anyone who has thought much about it, or tried seriously to act upon this commandment knows how very difficult it can be. Difficult to understand what it means and difficult to live it out when we do somewhat understand it.

Love is a much-used and much-abused word. We often use it to refer to our natural affection and preferences. But these natural affections and preferences are not love. Sometimes they help and support love: sometimes they get in the way of love and obstruct it. Love is not affection or sentiment. It is a matter of reason and will. To love one another, in the sense which the scripture means it, is to will the eternal good of one another, and to act in terms of that will.

But how can we do it? Our own needs, our own fears and affections and preferences, keep getting in the way of it. So needful ourselves, we can hardly see our neighbour's good and will it. We are too caught up in our own unruly wills and affections.

Well, the Epistle for today has something vitally important to say about that too. The starting point is God's love for us.

'We have known and believe the love that God hath to us. God is love; and he that dwelleth in love dwelleth in God and God in him. Herein is our love made perfect ....'

It is our knowledge of God's love for us that enables us to love – to will the good – of one another. It is the knowledge that we are loved absolutely – at the very heart of our being, which frees us from our own needs and fears. That perfect love casteth out fear.

God's love for us, God's good will for us – that is to say, God's grace – is the basis and starting point. The first half of the Church's year is devoted to the celebration of that supreme and life-giving truth. Herein is love, not that we loved God, but that he loved us. That is the basis, and we must never lose touch with it. But if we do know that, then we can love one another – we can will one another's eternal good, and act in terms of that will.

'Beloved, if God so loved us, we ought also to love one another.'

And therefore we pray in today's collect, for the help of God's grace – his love for us – that we may keep his commandments of love, and please him in will and deed.

Amen.

TRINITY 1/ PENTECOST 2

In this was manifested the love of God towards us, because that God sent his only-begotten Son into the world, that we might live through him. Herein is love, not that we loved God, but that he loved us, and sent his Son to be the propitiation for our sins. Beloved, if God so loved us, we ought also to love one another.

In the doctrine and practice of the Christian religion there are many important elements and aspects. We all agree, I suppose, that everyone should know a little bit about theology – something about the nature of God; something about the nature of the world God has created; something about humankind, our origin, our nature and our destiny – and so on. We all agree that we should know something about the Holy Scriptures and that the Word of God should be faithfully preached and obeyed; that we should all say our prayers regularly, for ourselves and for others. We all agree, too, that we should all have some part in the practical affairs of the Church as an organization. The teaching of the Christian religion to both children and adults must go on continually. Church buildings with appropriate furnishings must be built and maintained. Someone must raise money. Committees must be formed, synods must meet, and so on.

We all agree that these things are important, but sometimes most of us find ourselves asking whether all this really adds up to the Christian religion; does all this really go to the heart of the matter? The trouble for many of us is that there are so many different things which are important that it's hard to see the woods for the trees. We get caught up in some particular aspect of Christian belief, or some particular aspect of Christian work, and find it hard to see how this is related to everything else that is supposed to be basic to us as Christians. Consequently, it is necessary for us from time to time seriously to consider what it is that is fundamentally necessary to being a Christian – what it is that makes us Christ's people.

The answer to the question is very well expressed in our text from 1 John:

> In this was manifested the love of God towards us, because that God sent his only-begotten Son into the world that we might live through him.

God in love offers to mankind new life through Jesus Christ. This statement summarizes what the Church brings to our attention in the series of fasts and festivals we have just finished from Advent Sunday around to Trinity Sunday. We have waited in penitence and hope for the coming of our Lord – and we have seen him, the Lord from heaven – an infant wrapped in rags in a stable in an obscure corner of the ancient Roman Empire. We have witnessed his glory at Epiphany – his shining forth unto the nation of the world. We have watched him follow the way of sorrows to be crucified on Calvary on Good Friday – the lamb of God sacrificed for our sins. We have seen too the glory of the resurrection – his triumphing over death, coming with new life from the tomb.

And then at Whit Sunday the Holy Spirit descended in tongues of flame, upon the apostles, sending them out to carry the gospel of God to the end of the earth. And last Sunday, the Feast of the Holy Trinity – we offered our praise and thanksgiving to God, who has granted unto us the way of salvation.

All of this certainly constitutes the most wonderful story ever told – the mystery of humankind's salvation. But except for one factor, it would remain a story and no more. That factor is this – God sent his only-begotten son into the world that we might live through him; that we might receive new life in Christ. And so it is, that when we are made members of Christ – baptized into his body by water and the Spirit, when we are nourished with his body and blood on the altar, we receive the new life – the new beginning which is in Christ. This is the fundamental fact about Christianity without which all else would be nothing – Christ has won new life for us – and in the sacramental life of his Church we receive that new life and are nourished and built up in it – we are marked as Christ's people. It would not matter how many sermons we heard, how many prayers we said, how many conversion experiences we had, how many good works we did. Unless we have received Christ's new life – unless we are baptized with water and the Spirit – unless we eat the flesh of the Son of Man and drink his blood, we have no life in us.

On the basis of this new life in Christ, the whole structure of our life as Christians is built up – on this basis our faith grows and expresses itself in good works. The supernatural life of Christ transforms our natural life – gives it depth, meaning and destiny which it could not otherwise have. This supernatural life communicates to us as what we call grace, and it expresses itself in love.

And this is where the second part of our text fits in:

'Beloved, if God so loved us, we ought also to love one another.'

While we have received Christ's new life – and we must always remember that that is the fundamental fact about Christianity – we are marked as Christ's people – yet that new life can be stifled or even killed in us if it is not expressed. St Paul says that it is God who works in us both to will and to do his good pleasure – our whole life as Christians is in complete dependence upon God's continuing gift of new life – of grace. But in the same place St Paul exhorts us: work out your own salvation in fear and trembling. And so our new life in Christ must be expressed in love. If a man say, 'I love God', and hateth his brother, he is a liar. If we recognize God as the source and the end of our salvation, we must of necessity love our brother – created in the image of God, and called to the same salvation as ours.

This would seem to be a simple truth – but an astonishing number of professing Christians neglect it, or even deny it. There are thousands of Christians who have no worries whatsoever about political and economic systems which are responsible for the near starvation of a sizeable proportion of the world's people. There are professing Christians who have governmental policies on the principle that the white race is called by God to dominate the black. These and a multitude of other horrible perversions and denials of Christian faith exist in the world around us today. Surely, our new life in Christ expresses itself against all such things – it must express itself in love and in concern – sometimes in gentleness, sometimes in wrath – but it must express itself.

We who by the grace of God are Christ's people must

always be measuring ourselves and our world by the standard of God's love which he hath manifested to us. This calls for fresh decisions every day of our lives.

God has manifested his love to us in sending his only begotten son into the world that we might live through him. We must always give thanks and glory to God for this new life which is in our midst in the community of the Church, and within ourselves. But we must beware that we do not separate ourselves from that love of God, by failing to express in our life in this world that same love for our own fellow human. Only we ourselves, by our neglect and denial, can separate ourselves from the love of God. 'For I am persuaded', says St Paul, 'that neither death nor life, nor angels, nor principalities, nor powers, nor things present, nor things to come, nor height nor depth, nor any other creature, shall be able to separate us from the love of God, which is in Christ Jesus our Lord.' But we can and do separate ourselves – and so we must pray as today's collect bids us pray, for the help of God's grace, that in keeping of his commandments we may please him both in will and deed. And this commandment we have from him – that he who loveth God love his brother also.

Amen.

TRINITY 1/ PENTECOST 2, CORPUS CHRISTI

We have seen, and do testify, that the Father sent the Son to be the Saviour of the world. Whosoever shall confess that Jesus is the Son of God, God dwelleth in him, and he in God. And we have known and believed the love that God hath to us.

Today we begin the Sundays after Trinity, the longest season of the Christian year, during which the Church's lessons are concerned with the practical life of God's kingdom – God's kingdom within us, as individuals, and God's kingdom among us as a Christian community, as the people of God.

During the seasons of Advent, Christmas and Epiphany, Lent, Passiontide, Easter, Ascension, and Pentecost, we have recalled and celebrated the work of God for our salvation. 'We have seen, and do testify, that the Father sent the Son to be the Saviour of the world.' And in that sending of our saviour, we see, as St John says, the true nature of God as love. 'In this was manifested the love of God towards us, because that God sent his only begotten Son into the world, that we might live through him. Herein is love, not that we loved God, but that he loved us, and sent his Son to be the propitiation for our sins.'

'We have seen, and do testify.'

Our salvation, you see, is in the first place a kind of seeing, a kind of knowledge – knowledge of the love of God revealed, made manifest to us, in the work of Jesus Christ, by the mystery of his holy Incarnation, by his Cross and Passion, by his glorious Resurrection and Ascension, and by his sending of the Holy Spirit.

All this was summed up for us last week in the great festival of the Holy Trinity, that great festival of spiritual life, in which we celebrate God as absolute love: perfect knowledge of the eternal truth, and perfect will of the eternal Good. Knowledge of truth, and love of the Good, are perfectly one in God. That perfect unity of knowing and loving is God: the fundamental principle of our creation and redemption, the principle which orders and upholds all things in heaven and in earth, the principle which encompasses our lives with an ever-watchful providence. God is love: to know that, really to know that, is salvation, life, and resurrection.

And we do know that: 'We have seen and do testify.' We have seen the love of God in the sacrifice of his only-begotten Son. 'And we have known and believed the love that God hath to us.' The knowing, the contemplation, of that love, manifest in the sacrifice of Christ, is our means of grace and hope of glory.

Therefore, it is highly appropriate that the Thursday after Trinity Sunday, and sometimes this Sunday itself, is observed as Corpus Christi: a day on which our thoughts is especially focused upon the Sacrament of Christ's Body and Blood, that Sacrament in which the memory of his Passion is renewed, the soul is filled with grace, and a pledge of future glory is given unto us.

At the very heart of Christian life and worship, from the very beginning, in the New Testament, and all down the centuries, has been the priesthood and sacrifice of Christ: 'the one oblation of himself once offered', the sacrifice of his body broken, and his blood shed. In this sacrament, that sacrifice in which the love of God is manifest is made present to our minds and hearts under the visible signs of bread and wine, that the love of God may be our food and drink, and the pattern of our lives.

'We have seen and do testify.' Our salvation is in the first place a kind of seeing, a kind of knowledge of the love of God, revealed in the sacrifice of Christ. But we must testify to that knowledge, with our lips, and in our lives, and the lessons of these Sundays after Trinity will be all about that testimony. We must seek to understand, and conform our lives to the truth we have seen. One of the great theologians of the Christian Church, St Anselm, who was Archbishop of Canterbury at the end of the eleventh century, defined his understanding as '*fides quarens intellectum*' – 'faith seeking understanding'. We seek to understand the truth we believe, to conform our minds and wills to it, to make it the form and pattern of our thoughts and actions. From this standpoint, the work of Christian education is vitally important, in our Church Sunday Schools, certainly, but not just there. The task of Christian education, of ourselves and others, is the task of all of us throughout our lives.

This is not just a matter of information, not just a matter of knowing abstract doctrines, but of understanding Christian faith in such a way that it issues forth in Christian life: in charity, compassion, humility and patience, and all the other virtues of God's kingdom. The lessons for the Sundays after Trinity provide marvellous guidance for that sort of understanding, if we follow them thoughtfully and prayerfully. In fact, they present a magnificently ordered and coherent pattern of spiritual development, if we give them close attention. Perhaps the pattern is not always obvious or easy, but perhaps we should hardly expect it to be so. There is no instant spirituality that is worth very much, and we must be prepared to work at it.

I think we must recognize that much of our Christianity has been living – really rather parasitically – upon traditions which we have not worked very hard to understand; and we should not be surprised that such enfeebled belief and understanding easily fall victim to the secular attitudes which are so pervasive now, even in our churches. Vague goodwill, and conventions of respectability and liberality – attitudes which are themselves the shallow and diluted residue of Christian convictions – will not long sustain the fabric of Christian civilisation.

Perhaps the time has come to recognize more seriously, in the words of today's Collect, that 'through the weakness of our mortal nature we can do no good thing without God'. And then perhaps we'll be ready to finish the prayer: 'Grant us the help of thy grace, that in keeping of Thy commandments we may please Thee both in will and deed; through Jesus Christ our Lord.'

Amen.

TRINITY 2/ PENTECOST 3

This is his commandment, that we should believe in the name of his Son Jesus Christ and love one another, as he gave us commandment.

The message of the Church's liturgical year is a very simple lesson, and a very direct one: 'Believe in Jesus Christ and love one another', yet it seems to take us at least a lifetime to learn it. The essence of the message is summed up by St John in the epistle lessons for the first two Sundays after Trinity: 'In this was manifested the love of God toward us', he says, 'because that God sent his only-begotten Son into the world that we might live through him. Herein is love, not that we loved God, but that he first loved us, and sent his Son to be the propitiation for our sins.'

That is the first point of all our celebrations: that we should catch a glimpse of the manifest love of God, and be refreshed and elevated – 'reborn' – by that vision. 'No one has seen God at any time.' For the natural human, God is the great unknown, the power beyond, the mysterious principle of all existence. To know God in that way, as the infinite power governing the cosmos, is surely a noble knowledge, and also a tragic knowledge. But to know God as love is something far different. To know that eternal principle moving and governing all things as the divine love manifest is a transforming knowledge, a knowledge which changes us. To know that God is love is to see everything with new eyes, a 'new heaven and a new earth'; it is to be spiritually 're-born', to be saved from fear and hopelessness.

In Jesus Christ, the love of God is manifest: 'God so loved the world that he gave his only-begotten Son.' That is the starting point of our salvation, that we should believe that revelation of God's love; or, as St John puts it, 'that we should believe in the name of his Son Jesus Christ'.

That belief, that recognition, of God's love is the starting point: 'Hereby we know love, because he laid down his life for us.' We know love; and it is our destiny and vocation to be transformed by that love, to realise it and fulfill it in our lives. And there is St John's second point: our recognition of God's love is to be expressed in our lives with one another. Thus we are commanded to believe in Jesus Christ and to love one another.

And it is important to see that this transformation of ourselves in realising and expressing God's love is not something which just spontaneously happens. God's love is the seed of new life, sown in our souls, and it must be cherished, and nurtured and cultivated. Sometimes, alas, we give it only the barren and rocky soul of neglect; sometimes we choke it with thorns and thistles of worldly preoccupations, and the new life of the spirit withers and decays within us. That is the point of the parable of the Great Supper, in today's gospel: God's love is like an invitation; he bids us 'come, for all things are now ready; and they all with one consent began to make excuse'. Good excuses, no doubt, at least in worldly terms, and we could probably add to the list almost indefinitely. But with this invitation, no excuses will do. It is the Son of God who comes to call us to the heavenly banquet of God's friendship. Surely refusal is unthinkable; yet how often we manage to do it!

During this long season of Trinity, the concern of the Church's teaching is our response to that invitation: 'Come, for all things are now ready.' We are concerned with the nurture and cultivation of our new life, individually and institutionally. St John, in today's epistle, speaks of the signs of that life in us: 'We know that we have passed from death to life, because we love the brethren.' The love of God in us is manifest in our love for one another – our active goodwill and benevolence: not just in feeling, or superficial emotion, not just 'in word, neither in tongue, but in deed and in truth'. 'Hereby we know that he abideth in us, by the Spirit which he hath given us.' Our recognition of God's love has its necessary expression in our love of one another; and without that expression, we know that the recognition is counterfeit.

Thus we are commanded to believe the revelation of God's love in Jesus Christ, and commanded to express that love for one another. Perhaps it is one of the most surprising aspects of all this that St John keeps speaking in terms of commandments: we are commanded to believe in Jesus Christ, and commanded to love one another. To many of us, perhaps that seems a very strange way of putting it. After all, people either believe, or they don't; they either love one another or they don't. How can such things be commanded? The commandment to love seems especially strange: we're used to thinking of love as something spontaneous, something that just happens. It is an experience. One 'falls in love'. What sense does it make to command it?

But St John's approach is more realistic than our conventional modern attitudes about the spontaneity of belief and love. Our beliefs and loves do not simply 'happen';

they pertain to a character long formed by a long process of training and habituation. And that process always begins with commandment and obedience. Just as our natural life has its formation in obedience to parents and teachers, so our spiritual life has its formation in obedience to God's Word. There is of course a spiritual maturity, when our beliefs and our loves are spontaneously right. That is the condition we call 'sanctity'. But that is the end, not the beginning; our beginning is obedience and commandment, and the commandment is twofold: 'That we should believe in the name of his Son Jesus Christ, and love one another, as he gave us commandment.'

Amen.

TRINITY/PENTECOST SEASON AND THE LITURGY

The hour cometh, and now is, when the true worshippers shall worship the Father in spirit and in truth; for the Father seeketh such to worship him.

To many of our fellow Anglicans it would perhaps seem an exaggeration to say that the current crisis in the Anglican Communion is about liturgy. In a Church which seems lost in uncertainties about the most basic matters of theology, about the authority of Holy Scripture, about the unique lordship of Jesus Christ, and about the principles of Christian moral life, surely questions about liturgy, which seem so often to be questions more of style than of substance, must seem of very secondary importance. And yet, to think of the *Prayer Book* and liturgy in just that perspective would be to misunderstand both the significance of liturgy and the nature of the Anglican Communion.

Liturgy is after all the form of the Church's relation to God, in penitence, petition and intercession, in thanksgiving and adoration. At its centre is the thankful remembrance of the atoning sacrifice of Christ, and it looks forward with ardent hope to the liturgy of heaven: the new song of the redeemed at the marriage supper of the Lamb. All of these activities also have a place of course in the private devotions of every Christian, and publicly in various occasions of prayer and praise. Indeed, they are the daily life of the believer. But the Church's official liturgy is the common form and pattern, and in the liturgies pertaining to various stages and occasions of human life, the whole of our life is uplifted and set within the context of God's justifying and sanctifying grace. And it is within that context that the spiritual life of individuals and communities can grow.

It is important to recognize, however, that liturgy is primarily worship of Almighty God, 'our reasonable service'. Our own spiritual growth is secondary and consequential, a kind of by-product, a consequence of our focusing our love in God, and re-ordering all our loves in that perspective. That point may seem obvious enough; and yet, how much of contemporary liturgical theory and practice is predicated on the supposition that the primary purpose of liturgy is the building or improvement of our own spiritual lives or the life of our community, to such an extent that its God-ward focus tends to be obscured!

Increasingly secularized churches aim more at community building and world improvement than at heavenly beatitude, and liturgies are revised or newly-minted to reflect such preoccupations. Heaven fades from the Christian vision, and the new song of the redeemed gives place to the song of the modern city. In such a context, liturgy, in so far as it remains relevant at all, tends to be regarded as a device for encouraging psychological and social change.

But that is really not the point of Christian liturgy. The point of our liturgy, the meaning of our common prayer, is our entering, by grace, into the perfect self-offering of the eternal

Son to the Father; our entering into that adoring charity which is the life of God Himself.

> My God, how wonderful thou art,
> Thy majesty how bright!
> How beautiful thy mercy-seat;
> In depths of burning light!

The essence of our liturgy is precisely that ascent of mind and heart in loving aspiration; and all other aspects of our common prayer – our thanksgiving, our intercessions, our petitions, our penitence – all those aspects of our prayer are ancillary; always relative to the central focus of adoration, which is our union with God, our being in God, in and through the risen and ascended Lord. Our true liturgy resides in that adoring love which is the Son's relation to the Father; and the Spirit sweeps us up into that relation, when we begin our prayer, as Jesus taught us, looking towards 'Our Father, who art in heaven'.

Liturgy is not, finally, a means to any other end: adoration is itself the end and not a means, and adoration must always be the basic character and focus of our common prayer. 'The true worshippers shall worship the Father in spirit and in truth, for the Father seeketh such to worship him.' Thus, as Richard Hooker expresses it, liturgy constitutes a wondrous 'commerce' between earth and heaven:

> For what is the assembling of the Church to learn, but the receiving of angels descended from above? What to pray, but the ascending of angels upward? His heavenly inspiration and our holy desires are so many angels of intercourse and commerce between God and us.

God's grace descends to us, and all of creation, and ascends again in prayer.

Thus it is that Jesus, in today's gospel lesson, uses the miraculous harvest of the waters to point us towards a different harvest; the harvest of the spirit; the harvest of souls brought to maturity in him. 'Henceforth thou shalt catch men' – souls delivered from the barren and bitter waters of sinfulness and futility. What we are really concerned with is the everlasting life of the Spirit. Here we have no continuing city. What is saved is the harvest of the Spirit – spirits made deeper in knowledge and love of God, spirits made perfect in adoration.

'For the Father seeketh such to worship him.'

Amen.

TRINITY/PENTECOST SEASON AND MIRACLES

Thy faith hath made thee whole.

The Holy Scriptures abound in stories of miracles, from the beginning to the end, from the first instant of creation, when God called all things out of nothingness, when the spirit moved upon the face of the waters, and God said, 'Let there be light'. From the beginning to the end, when God will make a new heaven and a new earth: 'And I, John, saw the holy city, new Jerusalem, coming down from God out of heaven, prepared as a bride adorned for her husband … And he that sat upon the throne said, "Behold, I make all things new".' From the beginning to end, miracles of creation and re-creation. 'I am Alpha and Omega, the beginning and the ending, saith the Lord, which is, and which was, and which is to come, the Almighty.'

And between the beginning and the ending, there is the on-going miracle of existence and life and thought; for not an atom of creation and not a fragment of conscious life could for one instant continue if it were not sustained by that eternal thinking and willing which is God's providence. Even in our folly and perversity, we are held in life. 'It is by the Lord's mercy that we are not consumed; for his compassions fail not, they are new every morning.' The celestial orbs proclaim that providence: 'In reason's ear they all rejoice and utter forth a glorious noise. Forever singing as they shine – the hand that made us is divine.'

All that is miracle: the being and acting of God in the world: and it is in the context of that recognition that we should understand all the miracle stories in the Scriptures.

In our Scripture lessons this morning, we have two of those stories – one from the Old Testament, and one from the New; both about the healing of lepers, and they invite comparison. In the Old Testament story, Naaman the Syrian, overcoming his prejudice and pride, finally obeys the prophet's bidding, is healed by washing in Jordan, and comes to the awe-filled recognition that there is indeed a God in Israel. The miracle is a sign of the presence and power of God. That aspect belongs to the New Testament story also, of course: Jesus' healing of the lepers is a sign of the presence and power of God. But the New Testament story, and the miracles of Jesus in general, have still deeper dimensions which we ought to consider.

Jesus' miracles are signs of God's presence and power in him, the divine Son and Messiah. Remember how when John the Baptist, in prison, heard about the works of Christ, he sent two of his disciples to ask Jesus, Art thou he that shall come, or do we look for another? And Jesus answered and said unto them, Go and show John again those things which ye do hear and see: the blind receive their sight, and the lame walk, the lepers are cleansed, and the deaf hear, the dead are raised up, and the poor have the Gospel preached to them. The miracles are signs of Christ's messiahship and the coming of God's kingdom.

But the miracles of Jesus have a further dimension, when our attention is focussed not on the miraculous deed itself, but on its spiritual significance. Thus Jesus cured the blind and the deaf and the dumb, thereby signifying his power to open dull minds to the truth of God, and to rouse dumb spirits to speak God's praise. He feeds the hungry multitude, and shows that he is the true bread, the word of God, to nourish fainting souls. He heals the lame, and shows God's power to speed our pilgrimage to him. He stills the stormy seas of our confusions and despairs. He heals the sick and raises the dead, and thereby shows that he is our re-birth, our health, our resurrection to new and endless life in the Spirit.

Because the miracles are manifestations of the presence and saving power of God in Christ, we read the stories in the season of Epiphany: they manifest the power and wisdom of God for our salvation. But we read them again in the Trinity season, because they have yet a further dimension of meaning. As the first half of our Christian year sets before us what God in Christ has done for our salvation, so this second half of the year, this long Trinity season, is concerned with the realizing of that salvation in us, in the building up of our spiritual life as individuals and as community. That is the point of all our Scripture lessons in this season, and that is a dimension of the miracle stories: they are not only signs of what God has done and does for us, but also indicators of how the grace of God is fruitfully received in our lives.

Now, against that background let's think about today's two miracle stories, and compare them, and consider what they teach us about our own spiritual life. First, the story of Naaman, 'a mighty man of valour', commander of the army of the king of Syria. Naaman had definite ideas about how the healing of his leprosy should be undertaken. He set out for Israel with lavish gifts: ten talents of silver, six thousand shekels of gold, and ten festal garments for the king, and he came in a triumphal procession with horses and chariots to the prophet's door. To his dismay, Elisha didn't even appear, but sent a messenger to tell Naaman to go and wash in the Jordan. Naaman was enraged by the snub: '"Behold," I thought, "He will surely come out to me, and stand, and call upon the name of the Lord his God, and strike his hand over the place and recover the leper".' That was how it should have been done, according to Naaman. And as for Jordan, 'are not Abana and Pharpau, rivers of Damascus, better than all the waters of Israel?' Only when he puts aside his pride and preconceptions, and obeys the prophet's word, does he receive healing, as God's free gift, for which no talents of silver or shekels of gold could ever pay.

The ten lepers in the Gospel story are a step ahead of Naaman to begin with: they already know that their only hope of healing lies in God's mercy. They come to Jesus as beggars: 'Jesus, Master, have mercy on us'. Jesus tells them to go and show themselves to the priests: that is to submit to the elaborate system of examinations prescribed by the law, in Leviticus 14. But, of course, they are not healed by the Law, but by their obedience to Jesus' word. Their healing is God's free gift: *sola gratia* – by grace alone, here as also in the story of Naaman.

But there is something more in this New Testament story. Ten are cleansed, and only one of them returns to give glory to God, and he was a Samaritan – an outsider, with no claim upon the benefits of religion. Thus the story emphasizes still more sharply that salvation is not by the law, but by faith; by faith alone; and yet, as the Venerable Bede explains in his exposition of this Gospel, 'here we are shown … that it is not only confession of faith, but also the doing of the works that follow faith that makes whole those who believe, and gives glory to the Father who is in heaven.' The returning to give thanks is part of the healing – the evidence of it and the completion of it.

Finally, we should consider for a moment the implication of these stories for our own spiritual life, and, really, the practical application is pretty obvious: we come an outsider, and alien, with nothing in our hands to purchase our salvation, but only trusting in God's mercy to heal the leprosy of our sinful souls; we come, putting aside all pride of independence, and all preconception as to how God is to heal us, trusting only in his all-seeing wisdom. And we are truly healed when we live our lives always to the glory of God, in thanksgiving.

Therefore, as St Augustine says in one of his sermons:

> Let us give thanks to our Lord and Saviour, who without any previous merits of ours has healed our wounds, made us his friends who were his enemies, redeemed us from captivity, led us from darkness into light and recalled us from death to life; and humbly confessing our own infirmity, we implore his mercy, so that with mercy guiding us, he who has deigned to give us his gifts and graces may also deign to safeguard and increase them, who with the Father and the Holy Spirit liveth and reigneth world without end.
>
> Amen.

TRINITY/PENTECOST SEASON AND GLORY

Then shalt thou have glory in the presence of them that sit at meat with thee.

In this week's Gospel lesson we find Jesus' advice to socially ambitious dinner guests: When you are invited to dine at high table, don't rush headlong to the seat beside the President. He might have special guests, and ask you to move further along to make room for them, and think of the humiliation of that! Far better to go directly and conspicuously to the lowest seat. You might be asked to move up higher, and 'then shalt thou have glory in the presence of them that sit at meat with thee.' This is sound advice for glory-seekers, even if Jesus is making fun of them in giving it. But behind the fun of it, there is a serious meaning. The whole episode has rather the nature of a parable, and the point of it is summed up in the general conclusion: 'Whosoever exalteth himself shall be abased; and he that humbleth himself shall be exalted.' It's a parable about glory-seeking, and the right way to go about that. The point is that we are seekers of eternal glory, and we need to know how to attain it.

But just what is this glory? In Lewis Carroll's admirable work, *Alice Through the Looking Glass*, one of the main characters, Ovalius Crassus, offers a definition of 'glory.' He says it means 'a nice knock-down argument'. He has just enjoyed an argument about the superiority of unbirthday gifts, on the grounds they are given far more often – 364 days of the year – and he finds glory in his triumph. Alice is unconvinced by the definition. She claims that 'that's not what "glory" means'; and we'd probably share her skepticism. At any rate, a nice knock-down argument is only one sort of glory, and a very academic sort at that. And it had better not be eternal because it would be a particularly nasty form of hell.

The glory of the nice knock-down argument, like the glory of chief seats at dinner, does not amount to very much. These are just poor images of a higher glory, to which all desire of glory points, and short of which such desire never rests. Beyond all vain glories, there is a glory worth the seeking.

In modern times, 'glory' has become almost a bad word, especially if it is coupled with 'seeking'. There is a prevalent superstition that glory-seeking is a mean, unworthy business. Good people, and especially Christians, are supposed to be committed to service without thought of reward. We're not in it for the glory; we only want to serve. God's love is disinterested, and so is ours.

But that is very bad psychology, and even worse theology. It's important to notice a difference between us and God. God has no need of glory, but we do; in fact it's our most fundamental need. Our desire for glory, however stunted or distorted, however side-tracked into vanities, is at basis the desire for the vision of God, the knowledge of God as he is in himself. We desire to be 'partakers of that glory'; 'to perceive with open face the glory of the Lord, and to be transformed into the same image from glory to glory.' As St Augustine puts it, 'Thou hast made us for thyself, and our hearts are restless until they find their rest in thee.'

That is the desire of the whole creation, and the meaning

of its motion. The Greek philosopher, Aristotle, knew that the final cause moves all things as the end of their desire, and as St Paul explains, 'the whole creation groaneth and travaileth in pain together until now awaiting its adoption', that is, its resurrection to glory. What is dumb longing in the lower creature is in rational beings the rational desire for the glory of God, informed and clarified by faith and hope and love.

We are surely glory-seekers, and we must know how to do it. We have lots of devices for achieving vain glories, though there may be some question whether the game is worth the candle. In so far as real glory is concerned, we hardly know how to go about it. 'Sit down in the lowest seat', says Jesus. The point is that the glory of God is not something we can put together, or seize for ourselves. We have only the desire; the glory must be given. The lowest seat is the position of humility – the humility of accepting what we cannot achieve. That is to say, the beginning of glory in us must be the free gift of God's grace. 'Friend, go up higher.'

This gift of grace in us is the seed of future glory. As St Thomas Aquinas puts it, in his incomparably clear way: 'Grace has five effects in us: First, our soul is healed; second, we will the good; third, we work effectively for it; fourth, we persevere; fifth, we break through to glory.'

Our part is the thankful acceptance of God's grace, in word and sacrament, and in a thousand occasions of grace which surround us every day: in our work and leisure, in our associations with one another, in our troubles, and even in our sins. Through the manifold workings of his grace, 'may the Lord of eternal glory make us partakers of his heavenly table.' 'Then shalt thou have glory in the presence of them that sit at meat with thee.'

Amen.

THE CYCLE OF MARY

Duccio di Buoninsegna, *Maestà*, 1308-1311, tempera and gold on wood 84in x 156in, Museo dell'Opera Metropolitana del Duomo, Siena.

CONCEPTION OF THE BLESSED VIRGIN MARY

Hail Mary, full of grace: the Lord is with thee; blessed art thou among women.

Today we celebrate the Festival of the Conception of the Blessed Virgin Mary. In some parts of Christendom – in Quebec, for instance – this is a major festival and a public holiday. In our *Prayer Book* calendar, however, it has been demoted to black letter, or second class, status; because the event it celebrates is known to us from apocryphal rather than biblical sources. It celebrates the conception of Mary by Joachim and Anna. Mary's birth is observed in our calendar on September 8, also a black-letter day, and for the same reason: we have no biblical account of it. These, and other festivals of Mary, constitute an annual cycle, parallel to the cycle of festivals of Jesus; and in these cycles, the Feast of the Conception of Mary corresponds to the Feast of the Annunciation, the conception of Jesus.

Today's festival is sometimes called the 'Immaculate Conception'; and the term 'immaculate' perhaps needs some explanation. The word means 'unspotted', or 'unstained', and what the ancient ecumenical and classical Anglican tradition has in mind in the use of this word is that the human nature which the Son of God receives from Mary is integral human nature – that is to say, without the defect, the '*macula*' of original sin. As our proper preface for Christmas puts it, he was 'made very man in the substance of the Virgin Mary his mother; and that without spot of sin … '. The inference is that the mother who gives that perfect nature is also 'immaculate'. There is nothing particularly Romish or even 'High Church' about that notion: it is simply common Christian tradition. Mary is highly favoured, replete with grace, blessed among women.

But the modern dogma of the Immaculate Conception says something more precise than that. Although the dogma rests upon quite a long history, and has its *locus classicus* in the theology of Duns Scotus, it was promulgated only in December 1854, by Pope Pius IX, in the Bull, *Ineffabilis Deus*. And of course we mustn't believe anything as recent as that!

What the dogma states is that, 'Mary, at the first instant of her conception, by a singular privilege and grace of the omnipotent God, in consideration of the merits of Jesus Christ … was preserved free from all stain of original sin.' It says nothing about the manner of her conception by Joachim and Anna: only that from the moment of her conception, her nature was preserved from the defect of original sin. What the dogma actually amounts to is a theological explanation of how it was that Mary could be the mother of a perfect human nature; and it is quite a good theological explanation. But the Anglican Church has resisted making such theological explanations matters of necessary belief, and therefore the dogma of the Immaculate Conception is not for Anglicans *de fide*, but a matter of 'pious opinion'.

In modern Anglicanism, unfortunately, our Mariology seems to consist mainly of what we do not necessarily believe, and what we find 'unacceptable'. Unfortunately, I say, because it has been the experience of the Church that a sound Mariology is an essential concomitant to a sound doctrine of the Incarnation.

That is why, for instance, the great ecumenical Council of Ephesus (431), whose pronouncements are *de fide* for us, insisted upon the title 'Mother of God', in opposition to the heresy of Nestorianism; and that is why the Anglican divines of the sixteenth and seventeenth centuries insisted upon that same title against the fierce opposition of Puritans and Anabaptists. Anthony Stafford, for instance, in his book entitled *The Femall Glory*, loses patience with Henry Burton, his Puritan opponent, and remarks:

> The union of both natures, God and Man, being in Christ, [Mary] must, by strong consequences, bring forth God and Man. But Burton, and his silly fraternity, have not brains or a temper fine enough to distinguish between the Mother of God and the Mother of the Godhead, the first of which she truly is; the latter she is not.

The spirit of Classical Anglican thought and devotion in this matter is beautifully represented in John Donne's sonnet on the Annunciation:

> Salvation to all that will is nigh;
> That All, which always is All everywhere,
> Which cannot sinne, and yet all sinnes must beare,
> Which cannot die, yet cannot chuse but die,
> Loe, Faithfull Virgin yeelds himself to lye
> In prison, in thy wombe; and though he there
> Can take no sinne, nor thou give, yet he'll weare
> Taken from thence, flesh, which death's Force may trie.
> Ere by the spheares time was created, thou
> Wast in his mind, who is thy sonne and Brother,

Whom thou conceiv'st, conceiv'd; yet thou art now
Thy Maker's maker, and thy Father's mother;
Thou 'hast light in dark; and shutst in little roome,
Immensity cloysterd in thy deare wombe.

There is no doubt much in the tradition of Marian devotion which Anglicans generally find extravagant: the ecstatic prayers of St Bernard of Clairvaux; the quasi-erotic character of some medieval love songs to the Virgin; the emotional intensity of a Renaissance Pieta; and so on. Perhaps we find all that a bit rich for our blood. But perhaps also a bit of self-examination in regard to our own rather narrow modern provincialism in such matters would be useful, before we simply dismiss such expressions of Christian piety as 'unacceptable'.

At any rate, the great ecumenical tradition of Marian doctrine and devotion properly belongs to us as Anglicans, and it would doubtless be salutary for us, in both theological and sociological terms, if we could bestir ourselves a little more to join our classical Anglican forbears in celebrating 'the Femall Glory'.

'Holy Mary, Mother of God, pray for us sinners, now and in the hour of our death.'

Amen.

THE ANNUNCIATION OF THE BLESSED VIRGIN MARY, FIRST SERMON

Drop down, ye heavens, from above, and let the skies pour down righteousness; let the earth open, and bring forth the Saviour.

The heavens – plural: as though to indicate the three blessed persons; the Father sending, the Son taking flesh, the Spirit causing the conception. The skies raining down; picture the angel of the Annunciation coming from God, 'who maketh the clouds his chariot: who walketh upon the wings of the wind: who maketh his angels spirits'; the earth opening; 'our land shall yield its increase'. The Blessed Virgin opened herself to the privilege of grace, her mind to receive, her womb to conceive. 'Fear not, Mary: for thou hast found favour with God.'

The witness of the saints we celebrate through the Church's year constitutes a great spectrum of sanctity, in which the illuming gifts of the Spirit shine forth in all their marvellous diversity, dividing to everyone severally, as He will. And each of the saints manifests some essential aspect of that spectrum which is the wholeness and completeness of the spiritual kingdom, spread out for us through the cycle of the year, just as in wonderful images, Dante in *Paradiso* would have it spread out through all the circles of the heavens, and finally glowing in all its distinctions, in the radiating petals of the white Celestial Rose. By this discursive cycle of sanctity, we are continually recalled from our temptation to see it all too narrowly, our temptation to see one-sidedly only this or that pattern as authentic Christian piety. 'The wind blows where it will, and you hear the sound thereof, but you cannot tell whence it comes and whither it goes; so is everyone who is born of the Spirit.'

But in this graceful panorama of the Spirit's gifts, no doubt the festivals of Mary occupy a peculiar place and constitute a cycle of their own. For hers is not just one gift among others. As the Spirit-empowered bearer of the eternal Word, she is mediatrix of all the graces of the New Covenant. And thus she is the appropriate type and image of the whole Word-bearing Church, of the whole spectrum of the saints. Yet in our representations of Mary, it is inevitably some aspect of the wholeness of grace upon which we first focus, and in the Annunciation, I think it is the grace of humility that we are inclined to see first. 'Behold the handmaid of the Lord; be it unto me according to thy word.'

But when we look more closely, is it *really* humility that we see there? Or is it *only* humility that we see there? Certainly, what we see there has nothing in common with that soppy self-effacement sometimes called humility, which will trust none of the Spirit's gifts. But is it even humility in the *proper* sense of that word?

Humility is that virtue which restrains desire, lest it tend towards too great things in vain ambition. It is a virtue of restraint, and surely it is a great virtue. But is it really the dominant note in the Annunciation?

To Mary came Archangel Gabriel, with glowing

countenance, with gleaming robe, with wondrous step. And Mary said, 'Be it unto me according to thy word.'

Not so much humility, I think, as in fact its complementary opposite, magnanimity, greatness of soul; that virtue which impels the soul to what is great, that virtue which, as St Thomas puts it, 'does not shrink from glory'. Mary calmly accepts what is great beyond all imagining, and from Our Lady of the Annunciation we needs must learn, not so much restraint, perhaps, as *impulse* of soul. For surely we lie bound in a lethargy of sin and failure and fears, shrinking from glory.

> No! I am not Prince Hamlet; nor was meant to be;
> [. . .]
> I have heard the mermaids singing each to each.
> I do not think that they will sing to me.

Shrinking from glory; in the name of humility – that is the worst of it! Not to have hope of glory, not to dare to grasp the greatness of the promises of God, that is what is really sad beyond all sadnesses. Certainly to recognize our sins and failures, and to accept them for what they are, without prevarication, and to restrain our vain ambitions – all this is the quite necessary office of humility. But it is the necessary office of magnanimity to see that even our most pitiful weaknesses are in God's promises occasions of grace, and that as the spiritual progeny of Mary, we too are called to be bearers of the Word.

But how shall these things be? 'Fear not, Mary'; Fear not, O soul! 'For thou hast found favour with God.' 'Be it unto me according to thy word.' With that assent, the ice of ages begins to break up. The heavens drop, and pour down their showers of grace, and wintry earth thaws, and opens its furrows. Therefore, in mystical song, the Saviour says to Mary, and he says to the whole Word-bearing Church:

> Rise up, my love, my fair one, and come away. For, lo, the winter is past, … the flowers appear on the earth; the time of the singing of birds is come, … Rise up, my love, my fair one, and come away. Come away.

In the Name of the Father, and of the Son, and of the Holy Ghost. Amen.

THE ANNUNCIATION OF THE BLESSED VIRGIN MARY, SECOND SERMON

Drop down, ye heavens, from above, and let the skies pour down righteousness; let the earth open, and bring forth the Saviour.

The ancient Introit for this festival speaks to us of a double motion: the descent of the heavens, and the rising up of earth. It speaks of a world awakened and made fruitful by the Incarnation of the Word of God.

> As the rain cometh down, and the snow from heaven, and returneth not thither, but watereth the earth, and maketh it bring forth and bud, that it may give seed to the sower and bread to the eater; so shall my word be that goeth forth out of my mouth: it shall not return to me void, but it shall accomplish that which I please, and it shall prosper in the thing whereunto I sent it.

Thus the prophet Isaiah proclaimed the mystery of the Word of God: it is like the rain from heaven, which makes fruitful the parched and barren earth. God's Word goes forth into all the world, and causes that world to bear fruit in spiritual life, in words and deeds of truth and grace, 'seed to the sower and bread to the eater'. Thus a person lives most truly 'by every word that proceedeth from the mouth of God'.

But just what is this dropping of the heavens, this storm of grace; what is this Word that goeth forth? It is the inspiration of the prophet and the vision of the seer, expressed in human words; and thus we speak of scripture as the Word of God. But the Word of God, behind the words, is nothing less than God himself. 'In the beginning was the word', says St John, 'and the word was with God, and the word was God.' The Word is God's eternal and complete self-knowing, the perfect self-uttering, which is not other than God himself: it is 'the word of his power', 'the brightness of his glory, and the express image of his person.' The Word is, as our creed reminds us, 'God from God, Light from Light, Very God from Very God.'

The Word of God is eternal, and eternally begotten, the Word of God goes forth within the life of God himself. And the Word of God goes forth in all creation, for 'without him was not anything made that was made'. 'By the word of the Lord were the heavens made, and all the host of them by the breath of his mouth.' That Word is the life of every creature, and 'the light that lighteneth every man', in all the world, from the beginning. And in Redemption, the Word of God goes forth, to dwell amongst us in the flesh, 'that we might behold his glory, the glory as of the only-begotten of the Father, full of grace and truth'. Who but St John would have dared to say it: 'we have touched and handled of the Word of Life.'

The rain of grace descends, and the barren furrows of the earth open to receive the Word of God. The Word of God goes forth, in words and signs and sacraments, and is expressed in a myriad of vocations, as the spirit's gifts are divided, 'severally as he will.' There must be prophet and apostle, pastor and teacher, poet and healer, artist and craftsman, and all those walks of life we sometimes dare to call 'ordinary.' Only in our diversity – only in the whole spectrum – can we reflect and imitate the infinite goodness and unity of God. Only thus the Word of God in us fills all things, in every aspect of creation, and returns it all in praise. 'My word shall not return to me empty', says the prophet.

This festival bespeaks a double motion: the descent of the Word, and the rising up of earth in fruitfulness. And St Mary is, as it were, the fulcrum of that double motion. The rain of grace descends: Hail, thou that art highly favoured; 'Hail Mary, full of grace, the Lord is with thee.' And earth rises in response: 'Be it unto me according to thy word.' All this is the work of grace – *sola gratia* – yet grace presupposes nature, which it heals and elevates and transfigures. As Thomas puts it, 'Grace does not destroy nature, but perfects it.'

Mary's place in this is unique. As Romano Guardini says:

> No one is like her, because what happened to her happened to no other human being. Here lies the authentic root of all exaggeration about her. If people cannot be extravagant enough in their praises of Mary, and even say reckless and foolish things, they are still right in one respect; even though the means are faulty, they seek to express a fact the tremendous depth of which must overwhelm everyone who realizes it.

The role of Mary is, indeed, unique and we celebrate her uniqueness with thanksgiving: 'Blessed art thou among women.' Yet there is also there a paradigm which includes us all. 'When I heard thy salutation', says Elizabeth, 'the babe leaped in my womb.' The Incarnation of the Word – that mighty downpour from the heavens – is to open up the furrows of our minds and hearts, that the Word of God might be fruitful in us, that the eternal Son of God might take shape in us. 'I live', says St Paul, 'yet not I, but Christ in me.'

Amen.

THE FALLING ASLEEP OF THE BLESSED VIRGIN MARY

O daughter, blessed art thou of the most high God, above all the women of the earth. Thou art the glory of Jerusalem, thou art the joy of Israel, thou art the honour of our people.

Those of you who are familiar with the calendar of holy days in the front of *The Prayer Book* will have noticed that today is one of the Festivals of St Mary. *The Prayer Book* calls it The Falling Asleep of the Blessed Virgin Mary. It is more commonly known as the Feast of the Assumption. In any case, whatever we may call it, what it celebrates is the entrance into heaven of Mary, the mother of Jesus Christ our Lord.

Though we do not perhaps generally pay very much attention to it, that calendar of saints days and holy days is an interesting and instructive document. The witness of all the saints it celebrates throughout the Church's year constitutes a great spectrum of sanctity – of holiness; a spectrum in which the illuminating gifts of the Spirit shine forth in all their marvellous diversity, 'dividing to everyone severally as he will'. As St Paul explains it, 'To one is given by the Spirit the word of wisdom; to another the word of knowledge by the same spirit, to another faith by the same spirit; to another the gifts of healing by the same Spirit'; and so on – there are many different gifts – 'But all these worketh that one and the self-same Spirit, dividing to every man severally as he will.'

There is great diversity of gifts; but each of the saints manifests some essential aspect of that spectrum of holiness which is the wholeness or completeness of the spiritual kingdom, spread out for us through the cycle of the year.

Just as a ray of light, shining through a prism of glass or through a rain drop, is divided up into all the different colours of the rainbow, so the light of Christ is manifested in all the diverse graces of his saints.

By this great spectrum, this great cycle of sanctity, we are continually recalled from our temptation to see holiness too narrowly – our temptation to see one-sidedly only this or that particular pattern as genuine Christian piety. Remember how Jesus explains to Nicodemus in the Gospel of St John: 'The wind blows where it will, and you hear the sound of it; but you cannot tell whence it comes, and whither it goes: so is everyone that is born of the Spirit.' We are perhaps impatient with difference and diversity and opposition; but all the push and pull, all the balances and counter-balances of all the diverse manifestations of God's grace are joined together and reconciled, for 'they are all the working of that one and self-same Spirit, dividing to every man severally as he will'. That, I think, is the meaning of our calendar of saints and holy days.

But in this grace-full cycle of the Spirit's gifts, no doubt the festivals of Mary occupy a special place, and make a cycle of their own: for hers is not just one gift among many. As the Spirit-empowered bearer of Jesus Christ, the eternal Word of God, she is the bearer of all the graces of the New Covenant, and thus she is the appropriate image or symbol of the whole Church, of the whole spectrum of saints.

Amen.

THE LIFE OF HOLINESS

ST JOSEPH OF NAZARETH

And Jacob begat Joseph the husband of Mary, of whom was born Jesus, who is called Christ.

In the history of Christian piety St Joseph has always been a bit of a problem. To begin with, he seems to be very much at the heart of the Christian mystery. He's there at Christmas and Epiphany, and the Presentation. He leads the flight to Egypt to escape Herod's wrath, and he's there again in the one story we have of Jesus' boyhood, the story of the visit to the Temple when Jesus was twelve years old. But then we hear no more about him. And even in those stories of Jesus' infancy and childhood, his position seems pretty ambiguous, because it's made perfectly clear that he's not really the father of Jesus. Mary is the important one, and Joseph seems hardly more than a social convenience.

There is a good deal of legendary, apocryphal material about him, of course, and medieval preaching managed to make something of him by means of poetic imagination. The breviary for this occasion contains portions of a marvellous sermon by St Bernard of Clairvaux in which that ecstatic twelfth-century preacher finds a wealth of comparisons between this Joseph and the more ancient Joseph, son of Israel. That ancient Joseph, he says, sold by the envy of his brothers into Egypt, prefigured the betrayal of Christ; this Joseph, fleeing the envy of Herod, carried Christ into Egypt; that Joseph was given understanding in the mysteries of Pharoah's dreams; this Joseph, another dreamer, was given knowledge and participation in heavenly mysteries; that Joseph stored up grain, not for himself, but for all the people; this Joseph had the safekeeping of the living bread from heaven, for himself and the whole world. And so on. It's a wonderful exercise in poetic imagination, but I'm afraid that to the more prosaic modern mind, it all seems highly fanciful and even arbitrary.

That is, of course, our problem; and it seems that what we lose from the poetry of faith, we must somehow make up in the science of theology. And I think that from the standpoint of theology, the place of Joseph is fairly clear. The intent of the evangelists, especially of St Matthew, is clear: they are concerned, in the first place, to connect the birth of Jesus very formally and precisely with the life of family, tribe and nation. What is important for them is that he belongs to the house and lineage of David; and therefore Joseph is important. It all begins in the particularity of family and tribe and nation.

But it soon appears that those particularities cannot simply comprehend this new life: Jesus represents a life which transcends the limits of family and tribe and nation, a life which involves a new and different birth; 'you must be born again', he tells Nicodemus, a ruler of the Jews, 'the wind bloweth where it listeth, and ye hear the sound thereof, but ye cannot tell whence it cometh or whither it goeth: so is everyone that is born of the Spirit'. He embodies and initiates a new community of spirit which knows and lives for an end beyond the natural. It is a universal family, and he is 'the firstborn of many brethren':

> One said unto him, Behold thy mother and thy brethren stand without, desiring to speak with thee. But he answered and said unto him that told him, 'Who is my mother? And

> who are my brethren?' And he stretched forth his hand towards his disciples, and said, 'Behold my mother and my brethren. For whosoever shall do the will of my Father which is in heaven, the same is my brother and sister, and mother'.

The new life transcends all purely natural forms, and so Joseph, and all the particularities of family and tribe and nation are left behind. It is a universal kingdom of the Spirit, which knows and loves a universal Lord. Do you claim to be Abraham's children? I tell you 'that God, even from these stones can raise up children unto Abraham'. There seems to be a negation of all natural forms and institutions. In those terms, one should understand the heresy of Montanism in antiquity, the Joachimites and Spiritual Franciscans in the Middle Ages, the radical Anabaptists in the Reformation, and even the various anarchists of modern times. They all claim the freedom of the Spirit: 'the wind that bloweth where it listeth.'

But that is to see the life of the Spirit in a very one-sided, and therefore distorted, way. It is the work of the Spirit not simply to negate nature, but to form it, to transform it, and elevate it, to serve spiritual and universal ends. As St Thomas puts it with masterful precision: '*Gratia non tollit naturam, sed perfecit*' – 'Grace does not destroy nature, but perfects it.' Nature and natural human institutions are necessary moments in the Spirit's work; that is where it must begin – Joseph has his necessary place in the history of salvation.

And, therefore, those who would live the life of grace must care again for nature and for humanity's natural institutions, for that is where the Spirit's work begins, in all the particularities of family and tribe and nation. That is the truth that Joseph stands for. He is the patron of our nation, and we do well to honour him.

Amen.

THE NATIVITY OF ST JOHN THE BAPTIST

What went ye out into the wilderness to see? A prophet? Yea, I say unto you, and more than a prophet. For this is he of whom it is written, 'Behold, I send my messenger before thy face, to prepare thy way before thee.'

We know only a little, really, about St John Baptist, cousin of Jesus, fierce, uncompromising preacher, in the wilderness of Judaea, 'clothed with camel's hair, and with a girdle of skins about his loins'; John the Baptist 'at Bethabara beyond Jordan' – just on the border of the promised land; preaching the baptism of repentance, and the coming of God's kingdom. His is 'the voice of one crying in the wilderness: "Prepare ye the way of the Lord. Make straight in the desert a highway for our God".'

It is sometimes supposed that he might have belonged to one of the radical sects of ancient Judaism, such as the community of Qumran, which produced those remarkable documents rediscovered only a few decades ago, which we call the 'Dead Sea Scrolls.' That Qumran community was a group of pious people who had separated themselves from the mainstream of Jewish life, and had gone to live in caves in the wilderness by the Dead Sea, awaiting the coming of the messiah with intense and ardent expectation.

Perhaps St John the Baptist came from such a group. At any rate, he was one of those who, like Simeon and Anna in the Temple, watched and waited for the fulfilment of God's promises. He was a minister and steward of the mystery of the coming of the Lord: the mystery of the Incarnation and the sacrifice of the Son of God.

'There standeth one among you whom ye know not': 'Behold the Lamb of God', he cries, 'Behold him that taketh away the sins of the world.'

Thus St John the Baptist, by his faith and spiritual discernment, was witness to the Word made flesh, and prophet of our Saviour's Passion; and that holy witness to the coming of the Word and the sacrifice of Christ is taken up in the mission of the Church, where the coming of the Word of God to minds and hearts is made audible in words proclaimed and visible in holy sacraments – the signs of his kingdom and his presence in our midst. 'To give light to them that sit in darkness and in the shadow of death; To guide our feet into the way of peace.'

'Behold the Lamb of God. Behold him that taketh away the sins of the world.' In that acclamation, which the Church reiterates every day, is encapsulated the very essence of the Church's mission: the Church exists to point to Christ, to proclaim Christ crucified, the Holy Lamb of God. The Church exists to minister his Word and sacraments: his Word made audible and visible for the forgiveness and salvation of mankind; 'To give knowledge of salvation unto his people, by the remission of their sins, Through the tender mercy of our God, whereby the day-spring from on high hath visited us.'

St John the Baptist is the prophet of the mission of the Church, which can have its true existence only in obedience to the Word of God made manifest in Jesus Christ. The Church of God can have no other ground. No bishop, no committee, no taskforce, no synod can ever give it any substance other than that. The Church must live by a commission not of its own devising, but divinely given in the Word revealed: 'Behold the Lamb of God. Behold him that taketh away the sins of the world.' Behold, the Son of God crucified. In ancient times, that seemed foolishness to Greeks, and a stumbling block to Jews. And to modern people it is surely no less difficult.

We live in an age in which it seems to many that there is no objective ground in matters human or divine; that knowledge can be no more than a morass of arbitrary opinion, and love no more than the vagaries of emotion, and that therefore our religion must be something of our own devising, based upon and judged in terms of our own immediate experience, our feelings and opinions as individuals and communities. Thus questions of religion seem to be matters of taste, perhaps to be resolved by the imposition of majority opinion, which, recognizing no objective ground, can express itself only in a kind of bureaucratic totalitarianism. May God deliver his Church from such tyrannies of feeling and opinion, in which there can be no salvation, but only conformity to arid and graceless secularity.

'The voice said, "Cry." And he said, "What shall I cry?" "All flesh is grass, and all the goodliness thereof is as the flower of the field … the grass withereth, the flower fadeth; but the word of our God shall stand forever".' The Church must ever hear and heed afresh the witness of St John the Baptist 'at Bethabara beyond Jordan'. St John the Baptist knows that Jordan's stream cannot be crossed, that the promised land cannot be gained, except by a baptism of repentance, except by a radical conversion of mind and heart, in obedience to the Word revealed. It cannot be gained except by a conversion of mind and heart which turns our world upside-down and inside-out: 'Every valley shall be exalted, and every mountain and hill shall be made low, and the crooked shall be made straight, and the rough places plain.'

The Nativity of St John the Baptist

In a world distraught by secular incoherence and fragmentation, lost amid confusions of opinion and insatiable desires, pushed about by fantasies and fads, and every wind of doctrine, may God grant us a renewal of the spiritual gifts of St John the Baptist, to speak the sure word of prophecy, to point to Christ our Saviour, to direct our footsteps over Jordan to that promised land which is the only homeland of our souls.

For giving me desire,
An eager thirst, a burning ardent fire,
A virgin infant flame,
A Love with which into the world I came,
An inward hidden Heavenly love,
Which in my soul did work and move,
And ever ever me inflame
With restless longing, Heavenly avarice,
That never could be satisfied,
That did incessantly a Paradise
Unknown suggest, and something undescried
Discern, and bear me to it; be
Thy Name for ever praised by me.

This soaring, sacred thirst,
Ambassador of bliss, approached first,
Making a place in me
That made me apt to prize, and taste, and see.
For not the objects but the sense
Of things doth bliss to souls dispense,
And make it, Lord, like thee.
Sense, feeling, taste, complacency, and sight,
These are the true and real joys,

> The living, flowing, inward, melting, bright,
> And Heavenly pleasures; all the rest are toys:
> All which are founded in desire,
> As light in flame and heat in fire.

Amen.

ST ANDREW THE APOSTLE

And the walls of the city had twelve foundations, and in them the names of the twelve apostles of the Lamb.

T*he Book of Common Prayer* offers us a system for spiritual growth: an ordered system or pattern for the sanctification of our lives by the grace of God in Christ; a system which gives to the moments and occasions of our lives a spiritual dimension. *The Prayer Book* offers us a system for the sanctification of time, the sanctification of our days and years; and thus it includes a calendar – an annual round of feasts and fasts which give our year a spiritual dimension. Thus year by year, we celebrate the great festivals of Christ, and also the festivals of his saints, who are witnesses to, and exemplars of, his grace.

'And the walls of the city had twelve foundations, and in them the names of the twelve apostles of the Lamb.'

Throughout our Church year are interspersed festivals of apostles, beginning with St Andrew, the first-called; and now, today, as we keep the Festival of St Andrew, Patron of our Church, we have occasion to think about the meaning of apostleship, and the apostolic character of the Church.

'And the walls of the city had twelve foundations . . .'. The apostolic number is twelve – the number of completeness. The whole Hebrew people consists of twelve tribes, and in the new Israel, the Church, there are twelve princes. In the new Israel, the twelve are witnesses to Jesus' resurrection; witnesses to the transformation of the old Israel according to the flesh into a new Israel according to the Spirit: a spiritual kingdom of all tribes and peoples. And thus, in St John's vision of the heavenly Jerusalem, the sacred number is twelve: twelve gates, with twelve pearls and twelve angels, twelve foundations of precious stones, twelve fruits of the Tree of Life by the waters of paradise. And the number of the redeemed is one hundred and forty-four thousand: twelve thousand from each of the twelve tribes. The number is symbolic: it means completeness, perfection.

Twelve apostles: twelve foundations of the city. The apostles are sent into the world. That is what the word 'apostle' means: one who is sent. The Word of God is sent into the world in the mission of the apostles: 'Their sound is gone out into all lands and their words unto the ends of the earth.'

> Twelve poor men, by Christ anointed,
> Braved the rich, the wise, the great,
> All the world counts dear rejecting,
> Rapt in their apostolate.
>
> Thus the earth their death-wounds purchased,
> Hallowed by the blood therefrom,
> On her bosom bore the nations
> Laved, illumined – Christendom.

The Word of God goes forth: that is the mission of the apostles and the apostolic Church. Everywhere spiritual life is begotten and nourished – often unseen and unsung, but the Word of God is never wasted. 'My word which goeth forth shall not return to me empty' – thus says the Lord and so it is. Every fragment is gathered in, and treasured up: twelve baskets are filled, 'that nothing be lost'; all is treasured up in that twelve-gated city of which all the saints are living stones.

To speak of the Church as apostolic is to speak of the 'sentness', the givenness of the Church, the givenness of the Word of God. We can impede and distort and pervert the word, no doubt, and sometimes we are quite good at doing just that. To be sure, we have our treasure in earthen vessels – frail vessels; some of them unseemly, some of them even vile. We try to conform the Word of God to our whims and fancies, but the Word of God is beyond our vain imaginings: it is given, it is sent, it will have its way: the gates of hell cannot prevail.

It is easy – all too easy – to be cynical about the apostolic Church: sometimes it's difficult to discern its apostolic character – its 'sentness.' Well, there are distortions and perversions, certainly. But there is also an immense, incalculable harvest of spiritual good, at all times and places, in innumerable kindly and saintly lives, often in circumstances which would seem to defy all hope or expectation. God's ways are not our ways, and we had best be slow to judge. God's Word prevails; God's will is done.

Our festival today summons us to celebrate the triumph of God's grace in St Andrew and the apostolic company. Our festival summons us also to be mindful of our own apostolic calling – for we, too, are called and sent. 'Andrew first findeth his own brother, Simon, and saith unto him, we have found the Messiah (which is, being interpreted, the Christ), and he brought him to Jesus.' 'He brought him to Jesus.' There, you see, is our apostolic mission, as a parish and as individuals. And on such apostolic foundations, God's holy city is built.

Now, as we stand on the eve of a new Church year, let us renew our commitment to our own apostolic calling. 'Master, where dwellest Thou', asks the apostle. 'Come and see', says Jesus.

'Come and see.' Amen.

ST PHILIP AND ST JAMES THE APOSTLES WITH ST JAMES THE BROTHER OF THE LORD

Philip saith unto Jesus, 'Lord show us the Father, and it sufficeth us.' Jesus saith unto him, 'Have I been so long time with you, and yet hast thou not known me, Philip? He that hath seen me hath seen the Father, and how sayest thou, show us the Father?'

The title of this festival in our present Canadian *Prayer Book* is complicated and perhaps even somewhat cumbersome – 'St Philip and St James the apostles with St James the brother of the Lord, martyr', and perhaps I should begin by trying to clarify that title for you if I can. The St Philip we have in mind is not the St Philip the deacon, of whom we hear in the Acts of the Apostles, but rather St Philip of Betheseda, one of the twelve apostles mentioned together with St Bartholomew in the list of apostles in the synoptic gospels. Practically everything we know of him actually comes from St John's Gospel, where he is frequently mentioned in various connections, as in today's gospel lesson. For instance, he is instrumental in Jesus' calling of Nathaniel, he is associated with St Andrew in the feeding of the five thousand, and so on.

St James the apostle, in today's title, is not that St James the apostle who was the brother of St John, and son of Zebedee – whose festival is on July 25 – but James the son of Alpheus, sometimes called St James the Less, also mentioned in the lists of the twelve apostles. This latter St James, son of Alpheus, was traditionally identified with the first martyr bishop of Jerusalem and author of the epistle of St James, from which today's epistle is therefore taken. And because Alpheus was thought to have been a brother of St Joseph, St James the Less was identified as kinsman, or 'brother' (in a broad sense) of the Lord.

However, modern biblical scholarship has raised doubts about the identification of St James the Less with St James of Jerusalem and therefore our *Prayer Book* revisors decided to add St James, the martyr bishop of Jerusalem, kinsman of Jesus, as a separate name in the title of the festival.

So, we commemorate St Philip, one of the twelve apostles; St James the Less, also one of the twelve, and St James, first bishop of Jerusalem, whose martyrdom is recorded in the Acts of the Apostles.

Now, there is much that could be said of historical interest about these three saints, particularly about St James of Jerusalem, and his significant role in the earliest forms of Church organization; but that is not my purpose this morning. Rather, as my text indicates, I wish to speak about the gospel lesson for the festival, and especially about its theological significance.

The gospel is the opening passage of the Last Supper discourse of Jesus, from which come also the gospel lections for the third, fourth and fifth Sundays after Easter. In general, that discourse prepares the disciples for Jesus' departure – his death and resurrection – and promises them a higher consolation and sufficiency in the presence of his spirit. 'It is expedient for you that I go away', he tells them. Only in the removal of his external, particular, temporal, presence, will they be able to recognize his inward, immediate and universal presence as Spirit; thus, he says, their grief will be as the pains of travail.

The disciples were considerably bewildered by all this, as their questions and interruptions indicate. No doubt the discourse has a marvellous serenity to our familiar ears; but really, the questions have a quality of desperation about them. Notice St Thomas' outburst in today's gospel. 'We do not know where you are going – how can we know the way?' And then St Philip's desperate demand: 'Just show us the Father, and that will be enough.' Enough, indeed! In that demand, all the hopes and hopeless longings of religious consciousness and the spiritual strivings of countless ages are summed up: 'Show us the Father. Show us God. If we could just see God then everything would be plain and clear and certain; no more bewilderment, no more nagging doubts, no more of those dark agonies of disbelief. Show us the Father.'

But alas! No one has seen God; for God is a spirit and dwells not in temples made with human hands. Those who worship him must worship him in spirit.

But 'show us the Father', says St Philip.

If St Philip's desperate demand is rather astonishing, Jesus' response is surely incomparably more so: 'He that hath seen me hath seen the Father, and how sayest thou then, show us the Father?' In that statement of Jesus is a truth so astonishing that we can scarcely look at it – it is the utterly stupendous truth of the Word made flesh – the truth that in the person of Christ, the divine and the human, the creator and the creature, the eternal and the temporal, the spiritual and the material, have come together, so that this earth now bears not only the symbols, the messages, the footprints of God, but is his very presence.

'God's presence and his very self
An essence all divine.'

'He that hast seen me hath seen the Father.' That is the central truth of Christian faith, and everything we think and do and are as Christians is in some way an implication of it. The cycle of the Church year is an interpretation of it, and sometimes we look at one facet of it, sometimes at another. Just now, in Eastertide, we are concerned with the end of it, the conclusion towards which this divine incarnate activity moves. St Athanasius stated the matter rather paradoxically when he said that 'God became a human, that we might become gods.' The resurrection of Jesus is a kind of consummation of his incarnation. If the incarnation represents the enfleshment of spirit, the resurrection represents the transformation of flesh by spirit.

The resurrection, you see, is not an abandoning of the flesh, but a transformation, a saving of it, a redemption of it – nothing is lost. The seed which falls to the ground must die; but it is not abandoned to corruption; it is taken up into a new life. So it is with the resurrection, says St Paul.

The resurrection of Christ represents to us our own destiny and the destiny of our world. We who are risen with Christ are to be taken up into the divine life. For we too shall be changed. That which is born of the flesh is flesh – but ye must be born again. As we have borne the image of the earthy, so also shall we bear the image of the heavenly. Indeed, says St Paul, the whole creation groans and travails in pain, awaiting its adoption, the redemption of the body.

In all this, there is a message of particular importance for us in our time. We are all inclined to become pretty thoroughly enmeshed in the flesh, i.e., in the immediate concerns of our worldly life, in such a way that we cannot see through them and beyond them. To such an extent is this so that, to many people, I think even the Church seems to be just another worldly institution, having to do with worldly improvement of one sort or another.

But the world is not enough. The world is not enough. 'Show us the Father', says St Philip, 'and that will be enough.' 'He that hath seen me hath seen the Father', answers Jesus. Let us then see him; let us touch and handle the Word of life; let us be reborn and transformed by his presence until we too are truly risen with him.

Amen.

ST MATTHEW THE APOSTLE AND EVANGELIST

Jesus saw a man named Matthew, sitting at the receipt of customs: And he saith unto him, Follow me. And he arose, and followed him.

The story of the calling of St Matthew, as St Matthew tells it in his own Gospel, seems very sparse indeed. 'Follow me', said Jesus. 'And he arose, and followed him.' That seems to be all there was to it. But was that really all? Where was Matthew's resumé? We hear nothing of his special gifts or notable achievements: only that he was a customs man; and surely, in those days of the hated Roman occupation of the country, that was not much of a recommendation. And what was the job description? What on earth did Matthew suppose that Jesus wanted of him? And what of selection procedures? We hear nothing of meetings of committees: not even so much as an ACPO weekend? What are we to make of it? As St Thomas remarks, in his 'Lectures on St Matthew': 'It is objected that this cannot be, that at one word he arose and followed him'.

It seems that there must be more to it, and that St Matthew's modesty has left everything to our imagination.

There is a wonderful interpretation of the story in a painting by Caravaggio, dating from about 1600, in the Contarelli Chapel of the great Baroque Church of San Luigi dei Francesci, the French

Caravaggio, *The Calling of Saint Matthew*, 1599-1600, San Luigi dei Francesi, Rome. Oil on canvas 127 X 130 in.

Church, in Rome. The scene is set in a dark, inner chamber of the customs house, where Matthew and four companions are seated at a table, engaging in counting coins. There, in the centre of the group, is Matthew; obviously very much a prosperous man of the world, with his velvet jacket and beret.

But the solemn business of the customs house has just been interrupted by intruders: Jesus and St Peter, who by their clothing and their bearing, are clearly quite foreign to this scene. Two of the companions at the table pay no attention whatsoever: their eyes and their minds are totally and greedily preoccupied with the money. Two others, stupidly arrogant young dandies, dressed in silks and swords, with plumes in their hats, turn and stare at the intruders with insolent distain.

And there is Christ, with his arm outstretched, with his finger pointing steadily at Matthew. St Peter, at his side, who represents, no doubt, the Church, just begins to imitate the gesture. In Matthew's face are signs of wonder and astonishment; his hands and mind are now withdrawn from the business of the table, and he is just on the verge of rising up to follow Jesus. But what, really, is moving him, and leaving his companions apparently untouched?

Modern technology contributes a clue to the intentions of the painter. Radiographs of the canvas reveal that Caravaggio painted initially an eloquent, speechifying Christ, and later changed his mind. In the final version, we see a still, ascetical, quietly authoritative Christ, with outstretched hand, who says only, 'Follow me'. But what is perhaps most wonderful of all about the picture is the quality of light which flows mysteriously from an unseen source, and penetrates the worldly darkness of the scene. It is the light of revelation, the light of God's grace and glory, 'the light of the knowledge of the glory of God in the face of Jesus Christ'. It is that light, the finger of God, the word of God, which arrests and changes Matthew. Nothing more is needed: just the quiet words, 'Follow me'.

As Dante puts it,

> That light doth so transform a man's whole bent
> That never to another sight or thought
> Would he surrender, with his own consent;
>
> For everything the will has ever sought
> Is gathered there, and there is every quest
> Made perfect, which apart from it falls short.

So it was with Matthew. No resume and no job description: just the light of our Christ breaking in upon his mind and heart. 'He arose, and followed him.'

But what of those who did not rise and follow? Did not the light shine also on their faces? Why were the quiet words not equally addressed to them? Why is one called and not another? Terrible questions, certainly; and beyond them lies the mystery of divine election, grace, predestination. No one sees the light, no one hears the word, no one comes to God, except the grace of God move him inwardly. Yet, as St Thomas says, God moves free beings to move freely. God does not work violence upon his creature's will, and the other side of the question is always, therefore, the mystery of our own human liberty of choice. Preoccupied with worldly occupation, we can ignore the light, or harden our faces in disdain against the penetration of it. We can stop our ears against the word.

We, too, are called, and chosen, signed and sealed by water and the Spirit, as disciples of the Lord. 'Follow me' is his word to us. He spoke it long ago, and he speaks it still. But, as I'm sure we know within ourselves, that word is something we must hear continually, afresh each day within us, as we work out each day our own salvation, in the varied circumstances of our lives, amid the manifold temptations of greed and arrogance, complacency and vain ambition, the hidden things of dishonesty and craftiness, the world, the flesh, and the devil. Let our eyes be ever open to the light of grace and glory in the face of Jesus Christ, let that light shine in the inner chambers of our greedy hearts; let our ears be steadily attentive to his word.

We give thanks today for the calling of St Matthew, apostle, evangelist, and martyr. 'Follow me', said Jesus. 'And he arose, and followed him.' And let us pray, with today's Collect, that we, too, may be granted 'grace to forsake all covetous desires and inordinate love of riches'; that we, too, may truly follow Jesus Christ, and exchange the tawdry riches of our worldliness for the glory of his kingdom, of which this sacred eucharistic banquet is a foretaste and a pledge. Here is the assurance of our calling. Take and eat. Drink ye all, of this mystery of death and resurrection.

'Follow me.'

Amen.

ST PETER THE APOSTLE

Simon, Simon, behold, Satan hath desired to have you, that he may sift you as wheat. But I have prayed for thee, that thy faith fail not.

Our Christian year is punctuated by the festivals of saints: apostles and evangelists, martyrs and confessors; holy men and women, and children, too, of all times and places, of all sorts and conditions. These festivals set before us, in a splendid panorama, all the Spirit's gifts, the virtues and the graces of God's kingdom, in their marvelous diversity. They remind us, by their different emphases, that though there is 'one Spirit and one hope, one Lord, one Faith and one Baptism, one God and Father of us all', yet our holy calling is expressed in so many different ways. 'As the body is one, and hath many members, and all the members of that one body, being different, are one body; so also is Christ.'

'There are diversities of operations, but it is the same God that worketh all in all.' We have our unity in and through diversity. That is the pattern of the Church's life, and that is the pattern of all true social order: a gracious reciprocity of gifts and talents; unity in diversity.

Both sides of that are crucially important: both diversity and unity. All our diverse gifts have a common source, and must serve a common end; all express and serve a common faith. Thus this great festival of St Peter comes in the midst of the Christian year, as a festival of faith – that virtue upon which all the rest, all the gifts and graces of the saints, must hinge. All the rest must hinge upon that faith, that Petrine affirmation, 'Thou art the Christ, the Son of the living God.' That is the foundation of all the diverse Christian virtues, the ground of Christian unity, the 'rock' upon which the Church of Christ is built; all Christian life begins with that, and hinges upon that. And we who keep St Peter's festival must celebrate and share St Peter's faith.

But is such clear and confident assertion really possible for us? Amid all the complications of our lives, amid all the conflicting voices that assail us, from outside us and from within our own souls, can we be so definite as that? Surely, we think, surely it was easier for those first followers of Jesus. If we had heard Jesus teaching, if we had witnessed his miracles ourselves, surely faith would be an easy matter. So we tell ourselves.

But, you know, practically every page of the gospel contradicts that sentiment. Faith did not come easily. The lame walked, the lepers were cleansed, the blind received their sight, the dead were raised, and the poor had the gospel preached to them. The signs of divine presence were all there. But the people heard and saw as though they had neither eyes nor ears. They were disturbed, and cast about for explanation: 'He casteth out the devils through Beelzebul', they said, 'the prince of devils.' There was great popular excitement, to be sure, but the excitement served only towards Christ's rejection.

Even his closest friends hesitated when he asked them what they thought. 'Some say that thou art John the Baptist; some say Elijah, or Jeremiah' – some great prophet, risen from the dead. Yes, 'but whom do you say that I am?' It fell to Simon Peter – Peter the impetuous – to rise to the great affirmation: 'Thou art the Christ, the Son of the living God.' 'And Jesus answered, saying, "Blessed art thou, Simon, son of Jonas: for flesh and blood hath not revealed it unto thee, but my Father, which is in heaven".'

It wasn't easy and I don't think it became much easier. There at Caesarea Philippi, we see one side of Peter's faith: the moment of faith's clear affirmation: 'Thou art the Christ, the Son of the living God.' A little later, in Jerusalem, on the night of Christ's betrayal, we see another side. Still, there is the confident assertion: 'Lord, I am ready to go with thee, both to prison and to death.' But that very night, at the hour of cockcrow, there came the moment of denial: 'I know him not', said Peter, as he warmed himself by the fire. And the Lord turned, and looked on Peter, and Peter remembered how the Lord had said to him, 'before the cock crow, thou shalt deny me thrice'. And Peter went out, and wept bitterly.

All this, you see, belongs to Peter's faith: the warm, clear light of affirmation, the dark cold night of doubt and hopelessness, and then the tears of penitence. St Peter's faith is sorely tried and tested. 'Simon, Simon, behold, Satan hath desired to have you that he may sift you as wheat. But I have prayed for thee, that thy faith fail not.' And, in the end, the faith of Peter does not fail; in the end, it is affirmed again, in tears of penitence.

We who share St Peter's faith must also know and understand the trial of our faith. We walk by faith, you know, and not by sight. We see darkly, through a glass, as in a clouded mirror; we know in part. There is, indeed, the moment of confident assertion: 'Thou art the Christ, the Son of the living God', but there is also the moment of doubt, and manifold temptation, the moment of denial and betrayal, when we say, 'I know him not.' And then our Saviour turns and looks upon us, and faith returns, in tears of penitence.

I think it is vitally important that Christians nowadays should have some understanding of the meaning of the trials of our faith. Around us, not only in the world, but within the Church itself, and within our very souls, there are the pressures of insistent worldliness. The hosts of compromise and shallowness besiege the very rock of faith. 'Adjust, revise, conform', they cry. 'Surely thou art one of them', they cry, 'for thy speech betrayeth thee.' And how often, sorely tempted, do we reply, 'No, I know him not.' Then may we find the grace of Peter to shed the bitter tears of penitence.

St Peter shows us that there is no easy Christian faith. Trials and temptations, the dark night of doubt, confusion and uncertainty, are not just unfortunate accidents. In God's good providence, they belong to the very life of faith; for faith must be tried, like precious metal, 'which from the earth is tried, and purified seven times in the fire.' Do not suppose for one moment that we can avoid the testing. Indeed, as St James says in his epistle, we must 'count it all joy … knowing that the trying of our faith worketh patience.' 'Let patience have her perfect work', he says, 'that ye may be perfect and entire.'

Christian times are always times of trial. Perhaps those trials take different forms in one age or another, and different forms for each of us; but always they are, and must be there. Doubt and confusion – even the moments of betrayal – do not destroy the soul which is ready to return in penitence. What alone destroys the soul is the cold, hard cynicism, which blasphemes against the Spirit; which simply doesn't care. 'Simon, Simon, behold, Satan hath desired to have you, that he may sift you as wheat. But I have prayed for thee, that thy faith fail not.'

Cling to the rock of St Peter's faith, and 'count it all joy'; 'Let patience have her perfect work.' That rock will not fail us; we have our Saviour's promise that 'the gates of hell shall not prevail against it.'

Amen.

ST JAMES THE APOSTLE

Ye are built upon the foundation of apostles and prophets, Jesus Christ himself being the chief corner stone.

What a joy and a privilege it is to celebrate this festival of St James here in this parish, and in this lovely old church, dedicated in his honour; and I thank your parish priest most sincerely for this opportunity. We celebrate the festival of our patron saint, and we give thanks that here in this place, from one generation to another, the word of God has been faithfully proclaimed and his sacraments faithfully administered; that here, from one generation to another, many souls have been obedient to the calling of the Lord, and have borne faithful witness to the presence of his kingdom of the spirit in our midst. All around us in this building are the outward signs of that devotion – the 'outward robes of holiness', as Richard Hooker calls them. Here there is indeed a precious legacy of adoration. In this Patronal Festival, we celebrate that heritage with thanksgiving.

But, if we would truly make that heritage our own, we must ever think afresh, and understand anew, and for ourselves, the meaning and the mission of this house of God; and this festival of our patron saint is a splendid opportunity for such considerations, for in the Holy Scriptures, and in the Church's ancient liturgical tradition, the apostles are represented to us as the models and prototypes of the ministry and mission of the church. The word 'Apostle' means 'one who is sent', and the Apostles are sent forth as faithful witnesses to the fullness of the grace and truth of God revealed in Jesus Christ. And that, precisely, is the mission of the apostolic Church: 'ye are built upon the foundation of apostles and prophets, Jesus Christ himself being the chief corner stone.'

Today's collect makes the point very clearly:

> Grant, O merciful God, that as thine holy Apostle, St James, leaving his father and all that he had, without delay was obedient unto the calling of thy Son Jesus Christ, and followed him; so we, forsaking all worldly and carnal affections, may be evermore ready to follow thy holy commandments.

Of St James, in particular, we know only a little: called together with his brother John, he became one of the specially chosen three who were particularly close to Jesus, the three who were present with Jesus on many crucial occasions: for instance, at the raising of Jairus' daughter, on the Mount of the Transfiguration, and in the Garden of Gethsemane, on the night of Jesus' agony. Jesus nicknamed James and John 'Boanerges' – 'sons of thunder' – suggesting their ardent and impulsive zeal; and, perhaps because of his evident zeal, St James was singled out by Herod Agrippa, as we hear in today's lesson, to be the first martyr from among the twelve apostles – thus obtaining one of those places of honour in God's kingdom which he and his brother had desired as we hear in today's Gospel lesson: drinking the cup of Christ's suffering, and being baptised with the baptism of Christ's death.

Legend has particularly associated St James with the Church in Spain; and because multitudes of pilgrims, visiting his shrine at Compostela, on the Western coast of Spain, brought home scallop shells as souvenirs, the scallop shell has become his special symbol in Christian art.

But the chief lesson which we learn from this festival of St James is the lesson of today's Gospel reading. James and John came to Jesus, and asked him: 'Master, we would that thou shouldest do for us whatsoever we shall desire … Grant unto us that we may sit, one on thy right hand, and the other on thy left hand, in thy glory.' But, as Jesus explains, the assumptions behind their request are all wrong: they do not understand what the glory of God's kingdom is. They think it is like the kingdoms of this world; but, as Jesus tells them, further on in this tenth chapter of St Mark, the ways of God's kingdom are very different: its princedom and authority are of a very different kind. Its kingship is the kingship of a servant; its liberty is found in willing obedience.

The Church can have its true existence and its vital mission only in obedience to the word and will of God, made manifest in Jesus Christ and his sacrifice; it must live by a commission not of its own devising, but divinely given in the word revealed. The Apostolic Church must preach and live Christ crucified.

In ancient times, that was a difficulty, because it contradicted the assumptions and standards of this world: as St Paul remarked, it seemed 'foolishness to Greeks, and a stumbling-block to Jews'. And to modern people is it surely no less difficult. We live in an age in which it seems to many that there is no objective ground – no sure truth – in matters human or divine; that knowledge can be no more than a mass of arbitrary opinion, that love is no more than the vagaries of emotion, that the good is only what feels agreeable; and that our religion must therefore be something of our own devising, based upon and judged in terms of our own immediate experience, our feelings and opinions, as individuals and communities.

Thus questions of religion seem to be matters of taste, perhaps to be resolved by the imposition of majority opinion. May God deliver his church from such tyrannies of feeling and opinion, in which there can be no salvation, but only a conformity to the changing assumptions of the present age, a conformity to an arid and graceless secularity. 'Be not conformed … but be ye transformed by the renewing of your mind.'

The Church must ever be renewed, of course; and, indeed, renewal is a watchword in the Church just now. But we must think about what renewal really means. Genuine renewal is never a matter of tricks and gimmicks, never a matter of accommodations and conformities to the spirit of the present age, but depends fundamentally upon obedience to a higher truth revealed, and a higher aspiration of the human spirit; depends upon a vision of a higher, and a holier life, which challenges and contradicts our worldliness. The Church, in faithfulness to its apostolic calling, must stand against and contradict the spirit of the present age: 'It shall not be so among you', says Jesus to James and John, 'it shall not be so among you.'

Genuine renewal begins as we rededicate our own lives to penitence and adoration; genuine renewal begins as we are ready, as today's collect puts it, to forsake all worldly and carnal affections, and are evermore ready to follow God's holy commandments. Renewal of the Church, renewal of Christian community, renewal of our souls, does not depend upon, nor spring from, busy accommodations to the standards and assumptions of the world in which we live; it depends fundamentally upon obedience to the word of God, in a spirit of adoration. That is the spring from which will flow the Christian virtues of faith and hope and charity without which all else is 'sounding brass and tinkling cymbal'. That is the spring whose fresh waters will wash away the dull and dreary dust of worn-out worldliness.

The Church must hear and heed afresh the witness of our patron saint. An apostle is one who is sent, with a message from the sender. A martyr is one who witnesses to the truth of that message, even unto death. To celebrate the festival, as we do today, of an apostle and martyr is to be reminded that we too have our apostleship and martyrdom – for we, too, are sent – sent to witness to that new life which is God's kingdom within us and among us. That is our apostolic calling, and that is our sure foundation: 'ye are built upon the foundation of apostles and prophets, Jesus Christ himself being the chief corner-stone.'

Amen.

THE TRANSFIGURATION OF OUR LORD

We have not followed cunningly devised fables, when we made known unto you the power and coming of our Lord Jesus Christ, but were eyewitnesses of his majesty.

'Eyewitnesses of his majesty', says St Peter. He refers to the Transfiguration of our Lord Jesus Christ on Mount Tabor, when Peter, James, and John witnessed the vision of 'the light of the glory of God in the face of Jesus Christ'.

'His face did shine as the sun, and his raiment was white as the light.'

'He received from God the Father honour and glory', says St Peter, when there came such a voice to him from the excellent glory, 'This is my beloved Son, in whom I am well pleased.'

Today is the festival of the Transfiguration. It is one of the major holy days of the Christian calendar, but – I suppose, because it usually comes on a weekday, and in the midst of summer vacations, and so on – it tends to be very much neglected.

That is a pity, because it speaks to us of a profound and important element in the gospel message. It speaks to us of 'the light of the glory of God in the face of Jesus Christ.' 'We have seen his glory', says St John; 'we have seen his glory, the glory as of the only begotten of the Father, full of grace and truth.'

The glory of God is a fundamental theme of the whole of

the scriptures, from the beginning to the end. The glory of God is manifest in the works of creation.

'The heavens declare the glory of God', sings the Psalmist:

> And the firmament showeth his handy-work.
> One day telleth another: and one night certifieth another.
> There is neither speech nor language; their voice cannot
> be heard.
> Yet their sound is gone out into all lands; and their words
> into the ends of the world.
> In them hath he set a tabernacle for the sun; which cometh
> forth as a bridegroom out of his chamber, and
> rejoiceth as a giant to run his course.

In the majesty, the beauty and the mystery of creation, the glory of God is manifest, for those who have eyes to see it.

And the glory of the Lord is manifest, too, in the law and the prophets. When Moses came down from Mount Sinai, with the tablets of the law, his face shone, so that the children of Israel could not steadfastly behold it.

'And the glory of the Lord abode upon Mount Sinai, and the cloud covered it six days … And the sight of the glory of the Lord was like devouring fire on the top of the Mount in the eyes of the children of Israel.'

And the glory of the Lord is manifest in the visions of the prophets – in whirlwind, and earthquake, and fire – and in the still small voice. And Elijah the prophet, was caught up into heaven, in a chariot and horses of fire.

But the glory of God, manifest in the law and the prophets, comes to its fullness in Jesus Christ. That is why Moses and

Elijah appear with Jesus on the Mount of the Transfiguration. They are his forerunners: their mission is fulfilled in him. Thus the transfiguration sums up what has gone before. But it also points forward – it is a sign and prophecy of Jesus' resurrection and the final glory of his kingdom.

On the eve of Jesus' Passion, the chosen disciples are given a vision of glory; a kind of special foretaste, or anticipation; and therefore, 'Jesus charged them, saying, "Tell the vision to no one, until the Son of Man be risen from the dead".'

The glory of God is fundamental to the whole of divine revelation, and it should be fundamental in our own spiritual life. We tend to lose ourselves so easily in the pettiness of worldly things, and even our religious life tends to become petty and pedestrian. The Feast of the Transfiguration recalls us to focus our minds and hearts in the vision of God's glory – God's surpassing glory – 'the light of the glory of God in the face of Jesus Christ.'

In the gospel accounts, the Transfiguration is immediately followed by one of Jesus' miracles of healing. That is significant. What it means is that the vision of God's glory is the basis, the foundation of newness of life. If we lose that vision, we lose the mainspring of our spiritual life.

The Feast of the Transfiguration calls us to a renewal of vision – the vision of the Glory of God in the law and the prophets, but above all, the vision of the glory of God in Jesus Christ. Consider that glory – meditate upon that majesty, that beauty:

> My God, how wonderful thou art,
> Thy majesty how bright!
> How beautiful thy mercy-seat,
> In depths of burning light!

We are 'eyewitnesses of his majesty'. And, as St Paul says, 'We all, with open face beholding the glory of the Lord, are changed into the same image from glory to glory, even as by the Spirit of the Lord.'

Amen.

ST LUKE THE EVANGELIST

Though he slay me, yet will I trust in him.

We know St Luke first of all as an evangelist – the author of the third gospel – and also as the author of the Acts of the Apostles, the work which records for us the earliest history of the Christian Church. His gospel contains much precious material which we know only from St Luke: for instance, the story of the birth of John the Baptist, the story of the Annunciation, the story of the Presentation, the only story we have of the childhood of Jesus – his visit to Jerusalem at the age of twelve years, and so on. Three of our familiar canticles, the 'Benedictus', the 'Magnificat', and the 'Nunc Dimittis', are found only in St Luke's Gospel.

We know very little, however, about St Luke's own personal history. There is an ancient and widespread tradition that he was an artist, a painter of pictures, but the evidence is quite uncertain. But we do know, both from the Acts of the Apostles and from St Paul's epistles, that he was a companion of St Paul on missionary journeys. St Paul speaks of him with affection as his 'fellow-labourer', and 'the brother whose praise is in the gospel throughout all the churches'.

In the epistle to the Colossians, St Paul speaks of him as the 'beloved physician', and for that reason, St Luke has been traditionally regarded as the patron of doctors and nurses, and of the medical profession and the healing ministry generally. In recent years, the healing ministry has been receiving renewed emphasis in the Christian Church, and today, as we honour St Luke, it seems to me that we might usefully consider that subject.

In Christian history, the healing ministry has a long and distinguished record. Although medical science is in fact older than the Christian Church, and was cultivated, for instance, in ancient Greece, still, in late antiquity, and in the European Middle Ages, it became largely the province of Christian religious orders, whose members founded hospitals, and devoted their lives to the care of the sick. In modern times, and especially during the past century, our medical institutions have become gradually secularized: but still most of them can trace their history back to ecclesiastical foundations.

Nowadays, if one speaks of the healing ministry, I suppose many people are inclined to think particularly of the phenomena of 'faith healing', and the 'healing services' which now go on in many of our churches; but the healing ministry, properly speaking, must include, and our Christian concern must include, the whole vast range of healing work, whether it is directly under the auspices of the Churches, or not. And we should try to understand just what is the nature of our Christian commitment to that whole work of health and healing.

For Christians, the fundamental motive in all this is charity. We love one another, and we seek to bear one another's burdens, and to relieve one another's suffering. In charity, we will the eternal good of one another, and seek to free one another from any ill which may inhibit the pursuit of that eternal good. It is that care for one another that underlies the Christian's work of healing, not the assumption that sickness and death and worldly comfort are absolute goods. Sickness, if we can bear it with faith and fortitude, may be the occasion of great spiritual good, and death may be the gate of everlasting life. 'Fear not them which kill the body, but are not able to kill the soul', says Jesus: 'but rather fear him which is able to destroy both body and soul in hell.'

A world which has lost its sense of the soul's eternal destiny, a world which has lost its hope of heaven, readily fixes upon earthly health and longevity as though they were absolute goods, as though they were ends in themselves, as though an ever-lasting life of earthly health and comfort were our destiny. And what utter folly that is! As St Paul says, 'If in this life only we have hope, we are of all men the most miserable.' Preoccupied with health and worldly comfort, we engage in a soul-destroying pretense, and in the end, we lose both earth and heaven. Medical science makes splendid progress. We win a few more battles, and we live a few years longer, and in greater comfort than our forefathers did. That can be exceedingly worthwhile, if it means more opportunity to serve God in our neighbour, and train our souls for heaven. But we do not live forever, and we do not build an earthly paradise.

We seek to relieve the sufferings of others, and we face with trepidation our own sickness and death, and we thank God for every possible relief: not that these are absolute evils, but because they are tests of our faith, and who knows with what spirit we can bear them? Can we, like Job, praise God from the bottom of the pit? 'Though he slay me, yet will I praise him.' And so we pray, 'Lead us not into temptation', which means, 'Put us not to the test'. And yet the tests must come, and we pray that our faith fail not: we pray that God will 'deliver us from the evil one.'

'Though he slay me yet will I trust in him.' So said Job in his affliction. I know that someday, I will be sick, and that someday I will not get well again. I do not know, but I hope, that I will have the spiritual maturity to accept that with faith and hope. One of the finest statements I know of that spiritual maturity is in the beautiful lines of a great seventeenth-century Puritan divine, Richard Baxter. Here it is:

Lord, it belongs not to my care
Whether I die or live;
To love and serve thee is my share
And this thy grace must give.

If life be long, O make me glad
The longer to obey;
If short, no labourer is sad
To end his toilsome day.

Christ leads me through no darker rooms
Than he went through before;
He that unto God's kingdom comes
Must enter by this door.

Come, Lord, when grace hath made me meet
Thy blessed face to see:
For if thy work on earth be sweet,
What will thy glory be!

Then shall I end my sad complaints
And weary sinful days,
And join with the triumphant saints
That sing my Saviour's praise.

My knowledge of that life is small,
The eye of faith is dim;
But 'tis enough that Christ knows all,
And I shall be with him.

Amen.

ST MARY MAGDALENE

Charity shall cover the multitude of sins.

Today the Church keeps the Festival of St Mary Magdalene, and the scripture lessons appointed for today's services all have to do with her place as a witness to Jesus' resurrection. And she witnesses to his resurrection, not just because she was present at the empty tomb on Easter morning, and met the risen Christ in the garden, but also surely, because she was one whose life was made new in Jesus Christ. By her conversion of life, she witnesses to the resurrection, and proclaims new life to all who follow Jesus. 'Go and tell my brethren', he bids her.

We know very little with accuracy about St Mary Magdalene; but, in general, she is the example of a notable sinner who became a great saint. Just what her earlier life had been, we do not know precisely. St Luke remarks that seven demons had gone out of her. Probably she is to be identified with that sinful woman who crashed the Pharisee's banquet with an alabaster box of ointment and anointed Jesus' feet, and received forgiveness of sins. 'I tell you', says Jesus, 'her sins, which are many, are forgiven, for she loved much.'

'Charity shall cover the multitude of sins.'

St Mary Magdalene is a witness to the triumph of love. But what is this love, which wins new life, this charity which covers the multitude of sins? We can hardly mention the word 'charity' without recalling St Paul's great hymn of charity in the thirteenth chapter of 1 Corinthians, one of the best-known and most loved passages of scripture.

In chapter twelve of the first epistle to the Corinthians, St Paul writes to the Christians in Corinth about spiritual gifts – gifts of wisdom, of knowledge, of faith, of healing, of prophecy, of miracle-working, of administration, and so on. All these gifts are desirable, he says; but he will show us 'a still more excellent way' – the way of charity, without which all those gifts are worthless.

Obviously, we use the word 'charity' in a much narrower sense than St Paul has in mind. For us, it usually means gifts to the poor, or contributions to tax-exempt organizations, or perhaps a generous attitude towards somebody's foibles. Modern versions of the scriptures generally translate the word as 'love'; but it is doubtful whether that really goes very far towards clarifying the meaning of the passage. If the meaning of 'charity' has become too narrow, the meaning of 'love' has become too broad: so broad as to include even our attitude towards our favourite breakfast cereal.

We use the word 'love' to refer mostly to feelings and sentiments, to natural affections and preferences, and that is not really what St Paul is talking about at all. He is talking about a condition of reason and will, focused upon the eternal good, that is, upon God – a reason and will focused upon God, and in that perspective attending to the eternal good of one another. This is not principally a matter of affections or sentiments – it is a matter of perceiving clearly and steadfastly willing the eternal good.

Our natural affections and preferences are not charity, though they may sometimes be its accoutrements. Sometimes they help and support charity, and that is a happy circumstance. But sometimes they obstruct and distort it; and sometimes charity requires that our affections and desires be crucified:

because, far from seeking the eternal good, they are subjective and self-seeking. 'Charity seeketh not her own.'

Even in the resurrection garden, Mary Magdalene is tempted to cling to the earthly body of Jesus. 'Touch me not', he tells her, 'do not cling to me.' 'For I am not yet ascended to my Father.' True charity is to know and will the eternal good, to see beyond this or that particular earthly thing.

Without charity, says St Paul, all our gifts are worthless: sounding brass and tinkling cymbal – noisy nonsense – a cacophony of lifeless things, worthless: and it does not matter how much we know, or what wonderful and heroic things we do. Worthless because none of these gifts is finally of any use if we miss the end of all knowing and doing: the eternal good.

It is charity – the will perfected in its focus upon the good – which holds all things together towards that end. Charity 'beareth all things, believeth all things, hopeth all things, endureth all things.' Without that end, all things fall apart into a meaningless chaos, a mere series of episodes.

All our knowings and doings are parts: 'We know in part, and we prophesy in part.' But the parts make no sense without the pattern of the whole. They are like the pieces in a jigsaw puzzle – useless and ridiculous except for their place in the whole puzzle.

'When I was a child, I spake as a child' – I babbled – 'I understood and thought as a child.' 'But when I became a man', says St Paul, 'I put away my childish things.' It is the essence of childishness to hold to a part, a fragment, as though it were the whole. In childhood, the immediate, the particular object or objective is the whole world. To possess this or that, to taste this or that, to touch this or that, seems infinitely desirable, an end in itself.

To grow up is to see these things in perspective, to relate them to a perfection which is beyond this moment. 'Do not cling to me.' 'Touch me not', says Jesus to Mary, 'For I am not yet ascended to my Father.' She would cling childishly to his particular earthly form – he would have her espouse the absolute, eternal good which is God.

Charity is not gushing sentiment, nor is it indiscriminate affection or generosity. Charity requires rather the clearest possible discernment and discrimination of the good in every situation, and the most steadfast will in pursuing that good. Beyond faith and hope, charity is the ultimate mark of the maturity of the saint.

No doubt we are still children. 'We know in part, and we prophesy in part.' Our discernment is feeble; we see 'through a glass darkly' – vague and shadowy images of the good. We must pray and work for clearer vision and more steadfast will, that the new life of Jesus' resurrection may be perfected in us, that we, with Mary, may be witnesses of that resurrection.

Mary Magdalene, in the resurrection garden, through the midst of her tears, mistook Jesus for the gardener. But he is, after all, the gardener, who will cultivate in our barren soil the gifts and graces of his kingdom, and raise in us that best gift of 'charity which shall cover the multitude of sins'. And then we shall see him as he is, and know even as we are known.

'It will be said on that day, "Lo, this is our God; we have waited for him, that he might save us. This is the Lord. We have waited for him; let us be glad and rejoice in his salvation".'

Amen.

THE CONVERSION OF ST PAUL

I live, yet not I, but Christ liveth in me.

The Festival we keep today is not a very ancient one. The early Church observed a day in honour of the martyrdom in Rome of the chief apostles, St Peter and St Paul, and we still keep that festival at the end of June. But this festival of St Paul's conversion belongs to the Western Church alone, and began to be generally observed only in the twelfth century. Thus it is one of the many medieval accretions which so splendidly adorn our liturgy. It was introduced in the twelfth century – just at the point at which European Christians began to become deeply conscious of the historical dimensions of the Church's life.

And what more dramatic moment could the historian fix upon than the conversion of the Apostle to the Gentiles? One can think, of course, of other spectacular conversions of vast historical consequence. The conversion of the Emperor Constantine at the Milvian Bridge, the conversion of St Augustine in the garden near Milan, and so on. But all of these others hinge upon and depend so much upon the conversion on the Damascus road. St Paul was in some sense the father of the Gentile Church, and, in that same sense, the day of his conversion was its birthday. It was he, above all others, 'in labour more abundant than they all', who was the preacher of the Gospel to the world of Greece and Rome.

Brueghel, *The Conversion of Saul,* 1657, oil on panel 43in x 63in, Kunsthistorisches Museum, Vienna.

The Conversion of St Paul

St Paul has, of course, been blamed for much which certain critics have found offensive in the historical development of the Church. Those, for instance, who deplored the 'Hellenization' of the Gospel, traced the responsibility for it back to St Paul, who, in his speech on Mars' Hill had told the Athenians that he declared to them a God whom already, though ignorantly, they worshipped. Other critics, offended by what they regarded as excesses of Reformation theology, discovered the inspiration of it in what they considered extravagant Pauline language about 'salvation by faith alone.' In general, he has been blamed for corrupting with a mystical theology the original simple Gospel of the Jewish ethical preacher from Nazareth. He has been blamed for both Protestantism and Catholicism and perhaps we Anglicans can blame him for a combination of the two. But the fact remains that the letters of St Paul are our earliest recorded witness to the Gospel, and I'm afraid that efforts to discover a more primitive 'simpler' form of faith behind the Pauline complications have not shown much promise of success.

But it is the conversion of St Paul that must concern us now, and what are we to make of that? The blinding light on the Damascus road, and the voice that cried, for the hearing of Saul alone, 'Saul, Saul why persecutest thou me?'; and Saul of Tarsus, persecutor of the infant Church, became the Apostle Paul. No doubt, such a bare description of the incident leaves us dissatisfied; we'd like to probe the matter and say, in other terms, what really happened. But I think that Pieter Brueghel gets it right, in his great painting of this subject. Perhaps you remember Brueghel's peculiar habit of placing the real subject of his painting, not in the foreground or the centre, but in some remote corner of his canvas, to which the eyes of the viewer is eventually and inevitably drawn. In his painting of St Paul's conversion, there is at the back of the picture a mountain pass, at which a procession of men and horses has been halted in disarray. Some astonishing accident has taken place, but we can't see exactly what it is. That seems to be just right. The conversion of St Paul was fundamentally an inner thing, an event which can't be seen in itself, but only in its effects; it was the conversion of a soul.

St Paul himself regards it as a meeting with the risen Christ, who appeared, he says to him also, as to one born out of due time, and thus he saw his vocation and apostleship; that is to say, as witness to the resurrection, as witness to the living Christ. 'I live', he says, 'yet not I, but Christ in me.' And we can hardly improve upon that as a description of conversion, because conversion is not fundamentally a matter of blinding lights and secret voices, but a matter of a new integration of personality around a new centre, a new focus of insight and energies. 'I live, yet not I, but Christ in me.' It is death to an old life and resurrection to the new.

Much can be said and is said – endlessly, *ad nauseam* about the 'experience' of conversion, as though conversion were some sort of emotional orgasm. But high emotional temperature is no clear symptom of conversion. Conversion is, of course, experienced, and it does evitably involve revision of one's feelings, sometimes a revision long drawn out and painful, as one sees with St Augustine. But that is not the fundamental point. What is fundamental is that one's whole understanding and will be united in one principle understood and willed as altogether true and good. 'I live, yet not I, but Christ in me.' It is not a feeling, it is insight and vocation, 'casting down imaginations, and every high thing that exalteth itself against the knowledge of God, and bringing into captivity every thought to the obedience of Christ.'

What we celebrate today is the conversion of a soul, to find its life, its truth and its good in its living Lord; and as we do so, let us be mindful with St Paul himself of the broad dimensions of that conversion: it means not just the conversion of the soul itself but the vocation of conversion – the conversion of the Gentiles, the conversion of our social life to find the principle of that life in the charity of God; and indeed, the conversion of 'the whole creation which groaneth and travaileth in pain together until now', awaiting its redemption.

Conversion means the tuning and the forming of all existence towards its centre, source, and end in God. And the best of all acts and symbols of conversion is this very sacrament we celebrate, this sacrament of death and resurrection; this sacrament wherein Christ offers death and resurrection, earthly life in bread and wine, and here, by the word of God, they are converted – they are transformed – to be to us the life of God himself, that we may dwell in him and he in us.

'I live, yet not I, but Christ in me.'

Amen.

ST MICHAEL AND ALL ANGELS, FIRST SERMON

He will give his angels charge concerning thee,
to keep thee in all thy ways

It seems that nowadays angels have very little place in the intellectual and devotional life of Christians. Modern theologians are tongue-tied on the subject; empirical scientists cannot locate them among the revolutions of the heavens; astronauts have heard no rumour of seraphic wingbeats; and even the most pious believers are often inclined to consign the angels rather unthinkingly to the never-never land of fairy tales. To the modern mind, they seem to be figments of the imagination, having a certain appeal, perhaps, to romantic fantasy, but no genuine substantial reality.

What then are we to make of this Feast of St Michael and All Angels? It is, no doubt, a glorious festival; but what, really, is the cause of our celebration, and the object of our prayers? The collect for the feast speaks of that wonderful order in which God has constituted the services of angels and men, and has us pray that the holy angels who always do God's service in heaven may succour and defend us on earth. But who, or what, are these angels, and what is their divine service? What succour and defence can they bear us? What can we really know of angels and their doings?

The Scriptures, certainly, have much to say about them, they are there from the beginning to the end of the sacred history. They are there among the first works of creation, 'when all the morning stars sang together, and all the sons of God shouted for joy'; and they are there at the end, as the reapers, when 'the harvest of the earth is ripe.' They are there at the very heart and centre of it all, in the Annunciation to Mary, and at the Lord's Nativity. It is an angel clad in white who announces Jesus' resurrection, and white-robed angels attend his ascension. They are there in countless episodes throughout scripture, as God's messengers and ministers, in dress and appearance, to warn, to guard, to nourish and deliver.

Not only in our Sacred Scriptures, but throughout many centuries of the history of philosophical, theological, and scientific thought, pagan, Jewish, and Islamic, as well as Christian, the angels were the subject of profoundest commentary and speculation. They are the transcendent ideas of Platonic thought, they are the movers of the spheres in Aristotle's *Metaphysics*, and so on. The ongoing efforts to discern the nature and order of the angelic hierarchy are works of the greatest interest and importance for an understanding of the history of philosophy, and science generally, as well as of the practice of religion.

If we may presume to put all this in a nutshell, one may say, with Dorothy Sayers, that 'the angels represent the operations of divine providence: that varied and coordinated power imaging the whole spiritual order of the universe, quickened and sustained by the love of God.' They are pure intellectual substances, engaged everlastingly in the service of God's praise; and it is precisely that service of praise which sustains, succours and defends the spiritual order of the universe.

This point is beautifully made by that great theologian of

the English Reformation, the 'learned and judicious' Richard Hooker:

> God, which moveth mere natural agents as an efficient [cause] only, doth likewise move intellectual creatures, and especially his holy angels; for beholding the face of God, in admiration of so great excellency they all adore him; and being rapt with the love of his beauty, they cleave inseparably for ever unto him. Desire to resemble him in goodness maketh them unwearable and even unsatiable in their longing to do by all means all manner of good unto all the creatures of God, but especially unto the children of men: in the countenance of whose nature, looking downward, they behold themselves beneath themselves; even as upward, in God ... they see that character which is no where but in themselves and us resembled.

When we keep this festival of the holy angels, then, we celebrate those spiritual powers, those intellectual causes, on which the divine order of the universe and human life depends; we celebrate the agents of divine providence, according to which each creature in particular is the subject of God's care: that providence in which 'not a sparrow falleth without your heavenly Father'; that providence in which 'every hair of the head is numbered.' Each and every one of us is upheld and guarded by spiritual powers – we have our guardian angels. That is, of course, the point in the Gospel for this festival, when Jesus warns against offending the innocent. 'Take heed', he says, 'that ye despise not one of these little ones, for I say unto you that in heaven their angels do always behold the face of my father which is in heaven.'

In this festival, we are not concerned with fairy tales or figments of imagination; we are concerned to celebrate the providence of God in the spiritual order of the universe. We are recalled to associate ourselves with that mighty host and its chieftain, Michael, in the war against spiritual wickedness.

Not in flights of romantic fantasy, not in abstract curiosity, nor in occult bemusement; but in the immediate concerns of our relations to one another in a dispirited world, we are called upon to ally ourselves with the spiritual powers of God's providential care. 'Holy Michael, archangel, defend us in the day of battle.'

> Not where the wheeling systems darken
> And our benumbed conceiving soars! –
> The drift of pinions, would we harken
> Beats at our own clay-shuttered doors.
>
> The angels keep their ancient places; –
> Turn but a stone and start a wing!
> 'Tis ye, 'tis your estrangèd faces
> That miss the many-splendoured thing.

May your eyes be open to see God's glory in his angels; and Blessed be God who gives them charge to keep us in all our ways.

Amen.

ST MICHAEL AND ALL ANGELS, SECOND SERMON

Verily, I say unto you, Except ye be converted, and become as little children, ye shall not enter the kingdom of heaven.

We celebrate this week the great festival of angels, the great festival of Michaelmas, St Michael's mass. It is a great festival of praise for, as our collect reminds us, the angels who serve God everlastingly in heaven; and we, 'with angels and archangels, and all the company of heaven', we too are caught up in that wonderful order, that everlasting symphony of praise. And it is also a great festival of fortitude and hope, for as our collect also reminds us, the holy angels are messengers of God, appointed to 'succour and defend us on earth'.

But who, or what, are these angels? I could begin to answer, I suppose, with some of the definitions offered by the great philosophers and theologians of older times: angels are pure intellectual substances; they are the movers of the heavens; they are the everlasting spiritual principles by which the universe of God's creation is sustained and governed; they are the everlasting reasons, the pure ideas of things, hovering around the throne of God in adoration, ascending and descending to bind the earth and heaven in the wonderful order of a spiritual kingdom.

Such definitions are true, but perhaps they are not very

immediately enlightening. If we try to imagine pure spiritual beings, intellectual substances, inevitably we fail, for they exceed the material forms which imagination must draw upon. Artists of course have carved and painted angels: beautiful creatures, in human form, with wings to show they belong to a higher sphere than ours. And poets have tried to describe them. Dante, for instance, with his mind 'imparadised', lifts us to a glimpse of them:

> Thick as the sparks from molten iron sped
> So did the sparks about the circles chase …
>
> From choir to choir I heard Hosanna rolled
> To that fixt Point which holds them in their home,
> Hath held them ever, and shall forever hold.

But surely, that seems all fantasy, a dream of a very different world than ours. Who in our world, after all, encounters angels? Modern astronomers, it seems, have never met them; modern philosophers have no news of them; and modern theologians seem completely tongue-tied on the subject. If you were to tell your friends about your own encounter with an angel, I suppose they would be kind and understanding; and your psychiatrist would be interested to hear the details. The whole episode would be considered decidedly 'odd'. Angels seem to belong to a different world than ours; or at least to a very different perspective on the world.

How then, shall we celebrate these angels, who seem so remote and strange, and hard to understand? Jesus, in our gospel lesson, 'called a little child unto him, and set him in the midst of them, and said, "Verily, I say unto you, Except ye be converted, and become as little children, ye shall not enter into the kingdom of heaven".' Just what is he saying? First of all, of course, he is speaking of humility; and I think he tells us that the humble, wide-eyed wonderment of children is the road to discernment of the heavenly kingdom, the kingdom of the Spirit. 'If thy hand or foot offend thee, cut them off, and cast them from thee; if thine eye offend thee, pluck it out, and cast it from thee.' Only if you cut off the tired and cynical adult sophistication, which you possess or covet, only if you can cut off the offending hand and foot and eye: the hand that would grasp only the earthly good, the foot that would follow only the pedestrian paths of worldly wisdom, the complacent, sophisticated eye which is blind to any higher vision – only then, only when you are converted, turned around, to look in an opposite perspective, only then will you behold, with awe and wonder, that spiritual order which binds together heaven and earth in correspondence, that according to which, as Jesus says, 'the angels do always behold the face of my Father which is in heaven'.

When we keep this festival of Michael, 'warrior primate of celestial chivalry', we do not indulge in fantasy: rather, we celebrate those living principles of good, which inform God's natural and spiritual creation. This feast sets before us the context and dimension of our Christian conflict, which are so largely lost to us in the prosaic standpoint of modern secular religion. It reminds us, as the epistle to the Ephesians puts it, that, 'We wrestle not against flesh and blood, but against principalities, against powers, against rulers of the darkness of this world, against spiritual wickedness in high places.'

And it tells us that, in principle, that war is won. 'The dragon fought, and his angels, and prevailed not.' That war is won.

'They overcame by the blood of the Lamb, and by the word of their testimony' – διὰ τὸν λόγον τῆς μαρτυρίας – through the speech, the reason, the logic, of their witness, their martyrdom.

So sings St John, the seer of Patmos, as he gazes towards the open heaven. Ah, yes, and we too, if our eyes be open, we too shall see the heavens opened, and we too shall see with awe and wonderment the angels of God ascending and descending upon the Son of Man.

Amen.

ST CLEMENT OF ROME

Let all things be done unto edifying … For God is not the author of confusion, but of peace.

The Church Universal – both East and West – has traditionally celebrated Clement of Rome as bishop and martyr, but our 1962 Canadian *Prayer Book* calendar has robbed him of both those designations, in favour of the title 'Apostolic Man', whatever that means. It seems to me that our calendar makers were perhaps a bit carried away with the delights of historical criticism, especially in removing the title of bishop from Clement. It is just conceivable, though unlikely, that he was chief presbyter, or something like that, rather than bishop; but it seems rather finicky to remove a title which does have, after all, the support of a great deal of ancient and quite reliable testimony. So far as his martyrdom, in the Crimea, is concerned, the critics have somewhat better grounds; although the details of that martyrdom, and the miracles associated with it, are wonderfully depicted in Romanesque frescos in the ancient Church of San Clemente, in Rome, it must be allowed that the matter is historically obscure.

But at least St Clement has escaped the indignity of 'bracketing' which is what the calendar has done with 'certain ancient memorials whose historical character is obscure.' He certainly did exist, in Rome, in the first century, and certainly did write a long letter to the Church at Corinth, which we still possess. He is numbered among the 'Apostolic Fathers' – a group of seven Christian writers belonging to the first generation after the apostles, and some of whose works are actually contemporary with the later books of the New Testament. Clement's letter to Corinth, written in 95 or 96 AD, still exists, and there is no doubt about its historical authenticity; so I'll respect your critical sensibilities, and confine my remarks about Clement to the content and significance of his letter.

Compared to some of the more 'purple' passages of St Paul's epistles, the tone of Clement's letter is perhaps disappointing; gone are the fevers and chills of pentecostal fervour; with Clement – typically Roman, perhaps – all is calm and reasonable order. 'Since all this is clear', says Clement,

> and we have gazed into the depths of divine knowledge, we are bound to perform in due order all that the master bade us accomplish at the proper seasons. He ordered that the offerings and services should be performed at the appointed times and seasons, not at random and without order; and also by his own supreme will he himself appointed the place and the ministers of their performance, that all might be done according to his good pleasure and so be acceptable to his will … Let each of you, brethren, in his own order give thanks to God with a good conscience, not transgressing the appointed rule of his service, in reverence.

'Due order', 'proper seasons', duly constituted and authorized order of ministry, a sober piety: that is Clement's style and message throughout his letter. Not terribly exciting, perhaps; but, yet, there is something important there. There is a good sense of order and structure and institution, which is an essential dimension of Christian life. At the very heart of

Christianity, there is a certain tension: on the one hand, there is the immediacy of the Spirit, with its ecstatic freedom, the new wine of the Spirit, bursting the old wine skins of settled legal and religious and political forms and institutions. 'The wind bloweth where it listeth, and ye hear the sound thereof, but ye cannot tell whence it cometh or whither it goeth: so is everyone that is born of the Spirit.' So said Jesus to Nicodemus. 'Behold, the former things have passed away, Behold, all things have become new.' So said the seer of Patmos.

Yet, on the other hand, the creative Spirit is not the spirit of chaos, but of order; 'God is not the author of confusion, but of peace.' From the dark abyss of formlessness, he brings the order of nature and of human life. The divine Spirit does not simply shatter his earthen vessels, but transfigures and ennobles them to serve the highest ends. 'Grace', as St Thomas wisely observes, 'does not destroy nature, but makes it perfect.' Thus there is also a reconciliation between the Spirit and the forms and institutions of Christian life. God comes to us in a sacrament of bread and wine.

That tension, and that reconciliation, are problems of Christian life in every age. Think of the Montanists of the second century, the Spiritual Franciscans in the fourteenth century, the 'Radicals' of the Reformation, the revivalists and charismatics of modern times. Ever and again, they claim the freedom and immediacy of the Spirit, against all settled forms of Christian life. But a reconciliation is required: ecstatic tongues require interpretation. To the ancient Church of Corinth, St Paul has already spoken on this matter: 'For as much as ye are zealous of spiritual gifts, seek that ye may excel to the edifying of the Church … I will pray with the spirit, and I will pray with the understanding also … Let all things be done unto edifying …

For God is not the author of confusion, but of peace.'

The freedom of the Spirit, and the stable edifying forms – tension and reconciliation – that is a problem for every age. But it is especially the problem of the Apostolic Age when the ecstasy of the pentecostal spirit finds its first interpretation in the forms and structures of the Holy Catholic Church. St Clement, 'Apostolic Man', belongs to that history of tension and reconciliation. He has 'gazed into the depths of divine knowledge', and there he has discerned 'due order' and 'proper seasons' and 'appointed rule'; without due order there can be no community of faith, no Church, and no salvation. Thus we do well to give thanks to God for Clement, who was, no doubt, as our *Prayer Book* would have it, an 'Apostolic Man'.

Amen.

ST CLEMENT OF ALEXANDRIA

Destroy not the wise men of Babylon.

St Clement of Alexandria is not a very popular saint. There are no legends about him, no miracles, no heroic asceticism, no martyrdom. He was really only an academic, and, as everyone knows, academics don't make very good saints. His name appears in ancient church calendars, but both the Reformation and the Counter Reformation firmly abolished him, probably in consequence of the anti-Hellenic spirit which dominated the history of doctrine, both Catholic and Protestant, in Reformation and Post-Reformation times. 'Hellenizing' meant corrupting the pure Word of God by relating it to the worldly wisdom of the Greeks: and what more obvious 'Hellenizer' than St Clement, head of the Catechetical School in Alexandria at the end of the Second Century? Clement's works are full of appreciation for the doctrines of the Greek philosophers, and he even attributes to them a measure of divine revelation, parallel to the Old Testament.

Does his return to our Church's calendar in our 1959 *Prayer Book* herald a revival of Hellenism in the Anglican Church of Canada?

St Clement was certainly a Hellenist, but by no means an uncritical one. He saw in the wisdom of the Greeks a genuine dispensation of divine providence, a guide to righteousness, preparing mankind for justifying faith. The training of the Jews and the training of the Greeks were both providentially designed to fit mankind for the manifestation of God in Christ. Both were partial and imperfect, and were made more so by the imperfections of men. The various schools of philosophy, Jewish and Greek, says Clement, are like the devotees of Bacchus, who rend the body of Pentheus, and carry about the fragments in triumph, each one boasting that his morsel is the whole of the truth. But in the light of Christ, says Clement, all things are illumined, and those divided parts are united in a perfect whole, a perfect *logos*. In Christ, Jew and Greek are not opposed, but complementary. 'He hath made both one.' Thus, as Clement sees it, the Incarnation is the crown and consummation of the whole history of the world, and the supreme principle of inclusivity. 'Destroy not the wise men of Babylon.'

Formulated doctrines, Clement reminds us, are not ends in themselves; they are always partial. They are the means by which we rise through fragmentary propositions to a knowledge which is immediate and whole. Jew and Gentile have come by different roads; both providential, each a partial wisdom, and in Christ they have been made one and whole.

Clement himself was only an academic, and thus a rather one-sided saint. But perhaps even that one-sidedness should be celebrated. Aristotle remarks in his *Politics* that the principle of reciprocity is the salvation of the state. That is to say, the unity of the state is a harmony of diverse elements, each contributing from its own one-sidedness. The kingdom of God is like that too. As St Paul explains it, it's like a body which has many members with differing functions. But all are united in a common purpose and destiny. 'We, being many, are one body in Christ.'

The diversity of the saints exemplifies the principle of

reciprocity in the kingdom of God; and surely it's nice, especially in an academic community, to be able to celebrate a sanctity which is 'only academic.' In the Church, we are a great diversity, and, at our very best, we are all one-sided. We see parts of the truth, and we emphasize important things in one-sided ways. But in and through that diversity – and not without it – we are one in Christ; one in the community of reciprocity – the community of charity – which is the fellowship of the saints.

And in this age, in which many Church leaders are promoting a version of religious 'inclusivity' (as they call it), such as to abrogate the finality of Jesus Christ, perhaps St Clement can point the way to an authentically Christian inclusiveness, which can truly embrace the wisdom of the Greeks, and need not 'destroy the wise men of Babylon'.

'Destroy not the wise men of Babylon', says the prophet Daniel. Rather, let the star lead them from Babylon to Bethlehem, where the wisdom of all nations is summed up, and the desire of all nations is fulfilled.

Amen.

ST CECILIA

Whereupon are the foundations [of the earth]
fastened? or who laid the corner stone thereof;
When the morning stars sang together,
and all the sons of God shouted for joy?

The framers of our *Prayer Book* calendar, in 1962, in all the sublime confidence of liberal scholarship, bracketed the name of St Cecilia, on grounds of her historical obscurity; and now the draft proposal for a new calendar gives up bracketing, and proposes to omit her altogether. But we do well, tonight, I think, to gloss over the parentheses; or, better still, to treat them as points of emphasis rather than exclusion; for what this saint may lack on the side of positivistic historical precision, she more than makes up on the side of moral, aesthetic and theological significance. Patron saint of music, and legendary inventor of the organ, she moves our minds and hearts to celebrate the sacred music of creation and redemption.

In that celebration, the preacher has a modest, secondary role. The first place goes to music-making, and here tonight, that side of things is well attended to; to the preacher falls the task of helping us to think about the meaning of our music-making, the task of helping us to tune our thoughts to the musical theology of creation and redemption.

The world began with music; music was, and is, its deepest character: the concord of the heavens, the song of the angelic movers of the spheres, when God established the foundations, and laid the corner stone thereof; when the morning stars sang together, and all the sons of God shouted for joy. And the renewal of creation, the incarnation of our Saviour, brought the angel's song, the music of the spheres, to earth, that human ears might hear that song of universal peace and divine benevolence. 'Such music', says Milton (organist and poet), in his 'Ode on the morning of Christ's Nativity',

> Such musik (as 'tis said)
> Before was never made,
> But when of old the sons of morning sung;
> While the Creator Great
> His constellations set,
> And the well-balanc'd world on hinges hung.
> And cast the dark foundations deep,
> And bid the weltring waves their oozy channel keep.

And the world will end with music, when the angelic trumpet sounds, when the corruptible shall put on incorruption, and shall be changed, to sing the new song of the Spirit, in the consort of the blest.

It all begins with and ends with music. John Dryden says it beautifully in his 'Song for Saint Cecilia's Day, 1687':

> As from the pow'r of Sacred Lays
> The Spheres began to move
> And sang the great Creator's Praise
> To all the bless'd above,
> So, when the last and dreadful Hour
> This crumbling Pageant shall devour,
> The TRUMPET shall be heard on high,

The dead shall live, the living die,
And musik shall untune the Sky.

Music is the order of creation and redemption – the first and final order of God's universe, and music must therefore be the order of our lives. Thus Dante in the *Paradiso* shows us a vision of the saints, arranged in their diversity of virtues, and concord of their holy charity, according to the eightfold pattern of the planetary and starry spheres, according to the eightfold pattern of the scale of music, dissonance and consonance – the tonal qualities and reciprocal relations of note with note at diverse intervals.

Now all that, we say, was the business of imagination, poetic images; and images which have been drastically eroded by the changing sciences of astronomy and music. We no longer think in terms of singing spheres of the Ptolemaic universe, or the musical intervals of the Pythagorean scale. And that, of course, is true, at least to a great extent. And yet, good poetry is never just imagination; in and through eroded images, we may still glimpse the truth the poet's images expressed.

That truth, I think, is this: God's eternal truth, which we know, in part, by faith and understanding, is sensibly expressed in nature and in human arts, in diverse images of beauty, which have the power to move us to desire and seek our good in God, where the good, the true, and the beautiful are one. The divorces which we effect between the moral, the aesthetic, and the theological are finally untrue, and meanwhile disastrous for each of those bereft associates. They cannot do without each other.

Music, for instance, deprived of moral and theological perspectives, easily becomes just arbitrary acoustical experiment, just superficial entertainment, just one of those pursuits we nowadays call 'recreational'. St Cecilia protests! Music must be re-creational in a far more fundamental sense. Music, and the other arts, can find their true nature, their true freedom and integrity, only as they recognize their task as makers of the images of truth, whose beauty shows sensibly the grace of re-creation, and moves towards its everlasting good – that motion which also moves the host of heaven, 'all the sons of God', to shout for joy.

In the legend of St Cecilia there is a telling incident, beautifully described by Dryden:

> Orpheus cou'd lead the savage race,
> And Trees uprooted left their Place,
> Sequacious of the Lyre;
> But bright CECILIA rais'd the Wonder high'r:
> When to her Organ vocal Breath was giv'n,
> An Angel heard, and straight appear'd,
> Mistaking Earth for Heav'n.

There, precisely, is the spiritual significance of music, aesthetic, moral and theological: 'An angel heard, and straight appear'd/ Mistaking earth for heaven.' That is to say, the divine order of the virtues is clothed in images of sense, audible images which come to human ears. There are the angels – messengers of God; heaven comes to earth, that earth may come to heaven. It's the pattern of creation and redemption, the pattern of the sacrament; and that's what our celebration means: we celebrate the creative and redemptive grace of God in St Cecilia and the sacred music which she makes – the earthly echo of the music of the heavens.

Amen.

ST HILARY OF POITIERS

The mouth of the righteous is exercised in wisdom.

The ancient Gallic city of Poitiers, in Aquitaine, has many claims to glory, and a very special place in the memory of Christian Europe. It was from Poitiers, in 507, that Clovis, Frankish chieftain, converted to Catholic Christianity, set out to defeat the armies of the Visigoths, inspired by the miraculous portent of a pillar of fire rising from the Basilica of St Hilary. It was at Poitiers, in the year 722, that Charles Martel, mayor of the Merovingian palace, repelled the invading forces of Islam, and began to lay the foundations of Charlemagne's Holy Roman Empire. And Poitiers has many ancient monuments, among them the lovely early gothic cathedral, founded in 1162, by one of the most remarkable of medieval women, Eleanor of Aquitaine. Once married to Louis VII, King of France, she was now the wife of Henry Plantagenet (Henry II, King of England) and mother of Richard 'Lionhearted.'

Poitiers has many claims to glory: but brightest of all, and really the basis of all the rest, is not a warlord, nor a monarch, nor a monument, but Bishop Hilary, whose festival we celebrate today – first doctor, and first hymnographer, of the Latin Church. Fortunatus, the poet, described him as a 'bright lamp of nobility in the Gallic household' and Jerome, himself a doctor of the Church, called him '*Rhodanum eloquentia*', a Rhone river of eloquence. Born of a pagan family, he was well educated in rhetoric and philosophy, and was particularly devoted to the works of the Roman orator, Quintilian, converted to Christian faith by his reading of the scriptures. Soon after 350 he became bishop of Poitiers.

Hilary appears in the clear light of history for only about a dozen years – from 355 to 367 – but they were decisive years, and Hilary acted with sovereign efficacy. The mid-fourth century was the time of the most bitter doctrinal struggles of the early Church. Most serious of all was the heresy of Arianism, because that position denied the fundamental truth of God Incarnate – the Word made flesh – and thus would vitiate the whole conception of salvation. Some Arians said that Jesus was 'like' God; others said 'unlike' God; but all agreed that he was not really God. In a way, this whole issue had been settled by Constantine, in 325 at the Council of Nicaea, yet Arianism, in various forms, continued to flourish, supported by Imperial policy; and in the mid-fourth century, with the favour of the emperor Constantius, it reached the zenith of its influence.

Hilary boldly resisted the inroads of Arianism in Gaul, and protested vigorously against the expulsion and imprisonment of Catholic bishops. For his pains, he was himself expelled, and driven into exile in Phrygia, in Asia Minor. Despite what is sometimes said, one does not often find great theology done in exile; but Hilary is a notable exception to that rule, for his four years of exile produced the twelve books of his treatise *de Trinitate*, one of the fundamental theological works of Latin Christendom. Indeed, so effective was Hilary against Arianism in the East, that he was exiled back again to Poitiers, where he was received with great rejoicing; and it was largely through his efforts that the Council of Paris, in 361, declared in favour of the Nicene faith. What St Athanasius was to the East, St Hilary was to the West, and it was through the work of Hilary, more than any other, that Latin Christendom was first firmly committed to the orthodox catholic Christianity which gave its spiritual shape to western civilization.

It is tempting to try to give you Hilary's *de Trinitate* in a nutshell, but my *hubris* does not quite extend to that; so I shall content myself with just two quotations from it, and the rest you'll have to read for yourselves. The first quotation, from Book 8:13, concerns the Incarnation and blessed sacrament:

> If the Word was truly made flesh, and we truly take the word-flesh by means of the Lord's food, how can we not think that he naturally remains in us; he who being born as man assumed the nature of our flesh as now inseparable from himself, and has mingled the nature of his flesh with the nature of eternity under the sacrament of flesh which is to be communicated to us.

And, finally, the closing prayer of *de Trinitate*:

> Preserve, I pray thee, undefiled, this religion of my faith, and even to my last breath, grant that I may hear the voice of my conscience: that ever I may hold what in the Creed of my baptism I professed … that I may adore thee, our Father, and thy only Son; that I may win thy Holy Spirit, who is from thee, through thy only-begotten Son. For to me, a sure testimony of faith is my Lord Jesus Christ saying, 'O Father, all things thine are mine, and mine are thine' – my Lord Jesus Christ, in thee and from thee, God forever, and blessed unto the ages of ages.
>
> Amen.

ST JOHN CHRYSOSTOM

To you it is given to know the mysteries of the kingdom of heaven.

Many of the saints whom we celebrate in the course of the Christian year are very obscure, so far as biography is concerned; and sometimes we have to resort to hagiography, that very peculiar form of literature, which some of you, perhaps, find a bit rich for the blood. But with St John Chrysostom, we have no such problem: his career shines forth in the clear light of history. You can find a sober and accurate account, for instance, in the 33rd chapter of Edward Gibbon's *Decline and Fall.*

In the first century of the Christian Empire, Asia Minor produced a considerable number of great saints and scholars. One thinks especially of Basil of Caesarea, Gregory of Nyssa, and Gregory Nazianzen. It is with such names as these that one must associate John Chrysostom. Like Basil, his close friend, he was schooled under Libanius, the great pagan sophist, who was an intimate friend and correspondent of the emperor Julian the Apostate. Like Basil and the Gregories, he was educated in rhetoric, that most classical of disciplines, and was destined for a career in law. It seems that practically all of the greatest Greek saints of the late fourth century followed that same road. And with both St Ambrose and St Augustine, their contemporaries in the Latin west, the story was of course similar. All of them became bishops and doctors of the Church. It seems that Classics and Law made a very potent combination even in those days.

John was a great popular preacher in Antioch, and his golden rhetoric won for him his title, 'Chrysostom', which means 'golden mouth'. Hundreds of those magnificent sermons survive, as do also his biblical commentaries, which St Thomas Aquinas is said to have admired above all the glories of thirteenth-century Paris. When the episcopal throne of Constantinople fell vacant in 397, John was literally kidnapped by an imperial delegation, taken to Constantinople, and installed as bishop in the great imperial basilica of Hagia Sophia. That was in the days of the ineffectual and pious Emperor Arcadius, and the very effectual and not so pious empress, Eudoxia.

John's six years in Constantinople were stormy ones. He was caught up in the deplorable rivalry between Alexandria and Constantinople, and suffered much from the unscrupulous intrigues of the Alexandrine bishop, Theophilus. And, although he had an immense popular following in Constantinople, he was never very popular at court, partly because of his austere, ascetical character. I'm told that there is a legend that he always slept with twenty-three scrolls of Aristophanes under his pillow. If true, that would seem to be a spectacular demonstration of asceticism. At any rate, we know that he disfurnished the episcopal palace to found a hospital, and did no entertaining. He refused all dinner invitations, and insisted upon eating alone, said his enemies, 'like a Cyclops'. As Gibbon remarks, 'Although he struggled, according to the precepts of the gospel, to love his private enemies, he indulged himself in the privilege of hating the enemies of God and of the Church; and his sentiments were sometimes delivered with too much energy of countenance and expression.'

Certainly, he was lacking in tact. He boldly denounced corruption wherever he saw it, and even went so far as to call the empress 'Jezebel'. Relations with the imperial palace became decidedly cool, and the empress, with the aid of Theophilus and other enemies of John, after several abortive attempts, finally succeeded in exiling him to Cucusus, a lonely mountain village in Lesser Armenia. Despite the extreme hardships of his exile, he maintained a vast and influential correspondence; but after three years of shamefully bad treatment by his captors, he died, a confessor, if not technically a martyr.

From this story, G. L. Prestige draws the very Anglican moral that saints and reformers ought not to be made archbishops unless they are also men of sense and judgement. Be that as it may, I suppose it is not as an ecclesiastical administrator that we celebrate John Chrysostom, but as a doctor, and we ought to spend a few minutes thinking about what he teaches the Church.

What is most characteristic of the preaching of John Chrysostom is his uncompromising insistence upon the ethical demands of the kingdom of God and their universal application. One of the effects of the conversion of the old empire to Christianity, and the cessation of persecution, was an increasing worldliness in the Church. To many serious Christians, increasingly, it seemed that to seek the kingdom must mean to flee from the world; and the fourth and fifth centuries were the great age of that flight to the deserts. It seemed that only there, in solitude, one might strive for the perfection the gospel required. St Basil, indeed, recalled the monks from the desert with the question, 'If you live alone, whose feet will you wash?' He recognized the evangelical virtue of charity. And yet, for Basil, for Gregory of Nyssa, and for Gregory Nazianzen and others, the ideal remained the monastic life, and especially the life of solitary contemplation: the '*bios theoretikos*', they called it, the contemplative life.

John Chrysostom would have nothing to do with the double standard of the separated spiritual Christians and the ordinary worldly Christians. Although there are different vocations, the kingdom of God lays essentially the same demands upon all, whether monk or layman, whether the widow Olympias, or the empress, Eudoxia. The 'true philosophy', says John, can and should be followed by every citizen; only thus will cities truly become cities. There is a diversity of gifts, to be sure, and therefore diverse vocations. But there is one spirit, one hope of our calling. To the whole Church, not only to the monks, he holds up as a model the age of the apostles, 'where there was one soul and heart in all.'

It is a perennial temptation of the Church to decide that only one of the gifts, only one vocation, is the true one. Nowadays, I suppose we're not much tempted to think that it is contemplation. We're more inclined, perhaps, to think that it is social action, or ecstatic experience, or something else even less plausible. But John Chrysostom, the doctor, teaches us the great and wonderful mystery, that the kingdom of God is a city to which all gifts belong, that they are all gifts of the spirit, mutually enriching, and reciprocally completing one another. He teaches us that only in the community of gifts is the perfect life of heaven fulfilled, and that we are all equally called to that perfection. 'Blessed are our eyes' if we see that; for then, with Dante in the *Paradiso*, we shall see 'plain how Heav'n is everywhere/Paradise, through the grace of the First Good/ Falls differently in different regions there.'

Amen.

THE EXALTATION OF THE HOLY CROSS

Now is the judgement of this world: now shall the prince of this world be cast out. And I, if I be lifted up from the earth, will draw all men unto me. This he said, signifying what death he should die.

This festival of the Holy Cross, which we celebrate today, had its origins in Jerusalem, in the fourth century. It commemorates the discovery of the cross of Jesus, by St Helena, mother of the emperor Constantine, and the consecration of the great basilica which the emperor erected on the site. From that time on, the relics of the cross became a focal point of pilgrimages to the Holy Land, as we know, for instance, from a fourth-century document rediscovered in 1884, called the *Pilgrimage of Aetheria*, in which a Spanish lady gives a detailed account of her visit to Jerusalem in Holy Week, and describes the veneration of the cross.

From Jerusalem, the devotion spread throughout the Christian world, both East and West. We recall those marvelous hymns by Fortunatus, celebrating the glory of the cross:

The Royal Banners forward go,
The Cross shines forth in mystic glow.

Sing my tongue the glorious battle,
Sing the ending of the fray.

Those hymns were actually written in 569, to be sung in procession, as a relic of the cross was brought to Poitiers.

> O Tree of glory, Tree most fair,
> Ordained those holy limbs to bear,
> How bright in purple robe it stood,
> The purple of a Saviour's blood!

But how strange it is – on the face of it – that the cross should become for Christians the symbol of grace and glory. After all, for the ancient world, crucifixion was one of the most cruel and ignominious forms of death. Cicero, Josephus and Tacitus speak of it as the most atrocious form of punishment, reserved for slaves. The Romans used it especially for putting down revolts. In 67 B.C., Pompey had six thousand slaves crucified beside the roads outside Rome. Two thousand Jews suffered the same fate after the death of Herod the Great; and during the siege of Jerusalem in 70 A.D., hundreds of fugitives were crucified daily by the Romans. Such a death was doubly ignominious for the Jews, who recalled the pronouncement of the law in Deuteronomy, that he who hangs upon a tree is cursed of God.

How is it then that Jesus speaks of the cross as a sign of attraction and instrument of healing? 'I, if I be lifted up, shall draw all men unto me.' 'As Moses lifted up the serpent in the wilderness, even so must the Son of Man be lifted up.' He recalls that strange story in the Book of Numbers, in which the Lord commands Moses to make a brazen serpent and set it on a pole; 'and if a serpent bit any one, they would look upon the bronze serpent, and live.' Jesus took that image to himself. The Son of Man is to be lifted up upon the cross. We are to gaze upon his passion, with mind and heart, and in that vision of sacrificial love, our wounded spirits are to be healed.

There is in this a most remarkable reversal of perspective: wounds are a source of healing, death a source of life. The sign of shame becomes the sign of glory, for in this lifting up, the love of God is fully and finally manifest, and the true glory of the Son, the glory which he had eternally with the Father, is finally revealed. In the cross itself, the Son is glorified, even as he glorifies the Father in the perfection of obedience and love.

Thus Fortunatus sings:

> Fulfilled is now what David told
> In true prophetic song of old,
> How God the heathen's King should be;
> For God is reigning from the Tree.

'God is reigning from the tree.' A strange kingship, surely, and the world cannot comprehend it. 'Art thou a King then?' asks Pilate. A strange kingship, surely; here is no dominion but the monarchy of love; yet that monarchy endures when all worldly dominions are long gone in dust and ashes. The world has judged, and in its judgement, the world itself is judged.

Some of the implications of that great reversal are spelled out in today's gospel lesson: the story of the ambitious mother and her sons. They covet the seats of power in God's kingdom. But Jesus tells them that they do not understand. 'The princes of the Gentiles exercise dominion over them, and they that are great exercise authority upon them.' But the ways of God's kingdom are very different: 'It shall not be so among you: but whosoever will be great among you, let him be your minister, and whosoever will be chief among you, let him be your servant.'

The Exaltation of the Holy Cross

The glory of God's kingdom is the glory of the cross. By that cross, the world is judged, and the prince of this world is cast out. Now, as we celebrate the blessed memorial of our Saviour's death and passion, may we hold in veneration Jesus' cross; and may we ever strive to live beneath that holy sign.

Amen.

ST AUGUSTINE

Do not be conformed to this present age, but be transformed by the renewing of your mind.

This year, Christians throughout the world are celebrating the anniversary of the conversion of St Augustine. He was converted from paganism to Christianity in August of the year 386, so this year is the sixteen-hundredth anniversary. In a couple of weeks' time, scholars from all over the world will be gathering in Rome for an international conference to mark the occasion. And that will be followed by similar conferences in Philadelphia, Toronto, and other places. St Augustine was a very great philosopher and theologian, and scholars rightly pay him tribute. But he was, above all, a great and holy man, a saint; and he belongs, first of all, to the worshipping community of faith. So where better could we bring him tribute than right here, in the Holy Eucharist in this Church dedicated in his honour? He belongs, first of all, to those who hold the faith he held, those who cherish the holy sacraments he cherished, and those who seek to take, with him, the pilgrim's road to heaven.

The story of St Augustine's conversion is told in one of his own books, called the *Confessions*, a book which all of us can read, and re-read, with profit. The work begins as a sort of autobiography, in which he tells about his infancy and childhood, his education, and his professional career as a teacher. He speaks of the emptiness and frustration of it all, and the intellectual and moral confusions of his life in a world which had lost all sense of spiritual direction. It seems a very modern story in so many of its aspects.

The moment of conversion is described in Book VIII of the *Confessions*. The young Augustine, thirty-two years old, was seated in a garden, in Milan, with a copy of St Paul's epistles near at hand. Suddenly, he heard a voice, as though it were the voice of a child (like the refrain in some children's game), saying: *Tolle, lege, tolle, lege*: 'Take up and read, take up and read.' He took up the volume of St Paul's epistles, and read the first verse his eyes fell upon: 'Not in rioting and drunkenness, not in chambering and wantonness, not in strife and envying. But put ye on the Lord Jesus Christ, and make no provision for the flesh, to fulfil the lusts thereof.' From that moment, there was no turning back.

As the world regards such things, no doubt it was an obscure and unimportant moment. No doubt much more spectacular things were going on in the Roman army, and in the councils of the empire. Few people would have even known about it: Monica, Augustine's Christian mother, who had never ceased to pray for that moment; Bishop Ambrose, and the priest, Simplicianus, who had been helping him to understand the Christian faith; and perhaps a handful of his friends. An unimportant moment, as the world reckons such things; and yet, I suppose few moments can have been more decisive in the history of mankind. The Roman army and the Roman Empire would soon pass away, but the Christian Augustine, by his teaching and his writings, was one of the great architects of what we call 'Western civilization', and his works would shape the destiny of Europe for centuries to come.

Augustine wished to become a monk, to devote his life to study and meditation, but he was compelled to become a priest, and then a bishop, in the City of Hippo, in his native North Africa. There he died, in the year 430, as the Vandal invaders were besieging the gates of the City. In subsequent invasions, the City of Hippo, and, indeed, the whole great Church of North Africa, was destroyed and vanished as though it had never been. As though it had never been? Not quite: the holy lives and teachings of its saints have been immensely fruitful, by their influence, all down the centuries, to our own time.

But what of the teachings of St Augustine? There is no time now to speak about the doctrine of such great works as his treatises *On the Trinity* and *The City of God*, and his vast commentaries on books of Holy Scripture. His works occupy ten huge volumes, and just to list the titles would exhaust our time. But I want to try to tell you just one thing, and that's from the *Confessions.* At the outset of that work, Augustine speaks about the restless heart. Indeed, the whole of the *Confessions* is about that restless love, about the meaning of it, and the end of it; about the restlessness that directs our love to one thing, and then another, and then to something else, never satisfied, always longing for something more – something that will be perfectly true and beautiful and good. What is the meaning of that restless love? St Augustine explains it this way:

> By its own weight, a body inclines to its own place. Weight does not always tend towards the lowest place, but to its own place. A stone falls, but fire rises. They move according to their own weights, they seek their own places. Oil poured into water rises to the surface; water poured on oil sinks below the oil. They act according to their own weights, they seek their own places. Things out of place are restless. They find their places, and they rest.

> My love is my weight. Whithersoever I am moved, I am moved there by love. By thy gift, O Lord, we are set on fire, and are borne aloft; we burn, and we are on the way. We climb the ascents that are in the heart … With thy fire, with thy good fire, we burn and go on, for we go up to the peace of Jerusalem … There good-will will place us, so that we shall wish for nothing other than to remain there forever.

Our time is, as the time of St Augustine was, a time of worldliness, a time of restless, wayward loves. Worldliness invades the Church; worldliness corrupts our souls. St Augustine echoes the warning of St Paul: 'Do not be conformed to this present age, but be transformed by the renewing of your mind.' Worldly ends can never satisfy, and we must not be taken in by worldly hopes and expectations; that is to sell our true inheritance for a mess of pottage. We are made for something more than that: we are made to find our rest in God, and we will find it nowhere else. We must renew our minds in the Word of God; we must train our wayward loves by the daily disciplines of prayer and worship. We must habituate our souls to heaven.

That is St Augustine's conversion. By the grace of God, may it also be ours.

Amen.

ST DENYS AND ROBERT GROSSETESTE

Every good gift, and every perfect gift is from above, and cometh down from the Father of lights, with whom is no variableness, neither shadow of turning.

The festivals of saints interspersed throughout the calendar of the Christian year, set before us in a splendid panorama all the Spirit's gifts, the virtues and graces of God's kingdom in all their marvellous diversity. They remind us, by their different emphases, that although there is 'one Spirit and one hope, one Lord, one faith and one baptism, one God and Father of us all', yet our holy calling is expressed concretely in so many different ways. 'As the body is one and hath many members, and all the members of that body being many, are one body, so also is Christ.' 'There are diversities of operations, but it is the same God that worketh all in all.'

Our Saviour, Christ, is glorified in the chosen vessels of his grace, in every time and place. Just as a pure beam of light, passing through a prism of glass or precious stone, is made manifest in all the rich diversity of the colours of the spectrum, just so the grace of God in Christ is manifest in all his saints, according to all the diverse facets of character and nature, according to all the diversity of the Spirit's gifts, 'dividing to every one severally as he will.' And just as the beam of light is one, shining forth in all the colours of the spectrum, so the glory of the saints is nothing other than the one grace of God in Christ, the gift of 'one and the self-same Spirit.' Every good gift, and every perfect gift is from above, and cometh down from the Father of lights. Thus, as St Augustine says, 'when God crowns the merits of the saints, he crowns his own gifts.'

Today is traditionally the festival of St Dionysius, St Denys, patron saint of France, to which our *Prayer Book* calendar has added the commemoration of Robert Grosseteste, thirteenth-century bishop of Lincoln, and first Chancellor of Oxford University. The observance is further complicated by the fact that the St Dionysius commemorated is actually a conflation of three very different saints. First, there is Dionysius the Areopagite, converted at Athens by St Paul, of whom we are told in the Acts of the Apostles. Then, there is the third-century bishop and martyr, regarded as the founder of the Church of Paris, and commemorated especially in the royal abbey of St Denys, where his relics are still venerated. Thirdly, there is Pseudo-Dionysius the Areopagite, the unknown author of a remarkable collection of treatises on Christian Neoplatonic mystical theology. Probably he flourished in Syria at the end of the fifth century, but we know nothing for certain. It was in the ninth century, in the imagination of Hilduin, Abbot of St Denys, that those three distinct figures were merged into one, to constitute the multi-faceted patron of France.

The combination of St Denys and Robert Grosseteste in this festival is of course, a matter of historical coincidence: Grosseteste died on St Denys Day in 1253. But there are also considerations which would lift it above the level of coincidence. To begin with, Robert Grosseteste, learned in Greek, translator of works by Aristotle, Maximus the confessor, and John of Damascus, and commentator on those works, was also a translator of Pseudo-Dionysius' works, and wrote commentaries on Dionysius' treaties on *The Divine Names* and *The Mystical Theology*. This amounted to a re-introduction to the Latin West of an important source of mystical theology which would be profoundly influential in shaping the European mind in the late Middle Ages and in early modern times.

But Grosseteste goes well beyond translation and commentary, in a remarkable development of Dionysian dialectical theology of darkness and light. In Platonic tradition generally (as we see already in Plato's allegory of the sun in the *Republic*), light is the privileged metaphor for knowledge, darkness for unknowing, and the mystical theology of Dionysius involves an interplay of affirmation and negation, light and darkness, knowing and unknowing, which transcends all knowledge. Grosseteste works an astonishing transformation of that metaphorical pattern with a literal metaphysic of light, according to which light, as the most subtle of physical elements, has the central role in the production and constitution of the physical world. God said, *Fiat lux*: 'Let there be light. And there was light.' God's first creation is the self-diffusive point of light from which all the spheres of the cosmos radiate. (You can see whence Dante inherits the imagery of his ninth heaven.) Within the context of that metaphysic of light, Grosseteste develops an entire system of mathematical physics, and a science of optics, and becomes, in fact, the founder of experimental science.

Obviously, it is beyond the scope of a brief homily even to begin to explore the profound wisdom and vast influences of Bishop Grosseteste. The basic information is available of course in any history of medieval philosophy. To go beyond that calls for years of intellectual labour. To his contemporaries, Grosseteste was '*hom magnus in sanctitate vitae claritate sapientiae*': 'great in holiness of life and splendour of wisdom.' As we join in venerating these great doctors of the Church, it seems to me that we might appropriately gather our thoughts and devotions in that prayer with which Pseudo-Dionysius opens his treatise on mystical theology, Grosseteste's inspiration:

> TRINITY! higher than any being,
> any divinity, any goodness!
> Guide of Christians
> in the wisdom of heaven!
> Lead us up beyond unknowing and light,
> up to the farthest, highest peak
> of mystical scripture,
> Where the mysteries of God's Word
> lie simple, absolute and unchangeable
> in the brilliant darkness of hidden silence.
> Amid the deepest shadow
> they pour overwhelming light
> on what is most manifest.
> Amid the wholly unsensed and unseen
> they completely fill our sightless minds
> with treasures beyond all beauty.

Amen.

ST BENEDICT

For they that say such things declare plainly that they seek a country.

We celebrate today the grace of God in Benedict, 'Father of Monks' and 'Father of Europe'. Extravagant epithets, perhaps: after all, there had been monks for several centuries before Benedict. Since the late third century, the Egyptian desert had been fruitful with the prayers of the hermits, and in the fourth and fifth centuries monastic communities had flourished in East and West. Benedict seems more a conclusion than a beginning of that remarkable phenomenon. So, how is he 'Father of Monks'? And how is he 'Father of Europe'? Europe had so many and such complex sources: intellectually, perhaps, they come together in Augustine, or Boethius; practically, they come together in Charlemagne. How then is Benedict the 'Father'?

To understand the peculiar genius and sanctity of Benedict, we must begin by thinking of him in the context of his times. He was born about 480, in the little town of Nursia, in the Sabine Hills, fifty years after the death of Augustine, contemporary with Boethius and Cassiodorus, before the conversion of Clovis and the Franks, before the establishment of Theodoric's monarchy in Ravenna: a significant moment in the lingering death of an old order and the long, drawn-out birth-pangs of something new.

Gregory the Great, upon whose *Dialogues* we depend almost exclusively for our knowledge of Benedict, tells us how the young scholar went to Rome for the usual higher education in the seven liberal arts. Like Augustine before him, he rebelled against the sophistries and pedantic minutiae of those studies – mad Neronian fiddling while Rome burned – and left to seek a place of solitude. 'Full of ignorant learning', says Gregory, 'and wise where he was not taught.'

Still today, you can see that place of refuge: a cave in the cliffs at Subiaco, high above the river Anio, about forty miles from Rome, now adorned with medieval chapels, plastered against the cliffs like swallows' nests. Petrarch, visiting the place, thought himself to be on the 'thresh-hold of Paradise'; paradisal for Benedict, too, no doubt, but only in its utter solitude and austerity. Out of that background the Benedictine idea was born; and Benedict was nearly fifty when the first stones of his great monastery on Monte Cassino were laid.

The ideal was not that of a hermit, who flees the world for solitary struggle: it was rather the creation of a new world, a new city, in which all the trappings of the old – all the distinctions of rich and poor, peasant and noble, Roman and barbarian – were cast away; a city into which none could be born by nature, but only by grace and perseverance; a voluntary city, united and governed by a common end: the *Opus Dei*, the work of God, the praise of God. It was a society of common vocation, with distinction of function prescribed only by common need and differences of talent. That was the peculiar genius of Benedict. 'They that say such things declare plainly that they seek a country.'

'Father of Monks' and 'Father of Europe': what do we celebrate? To some, these phrases will suggest a blend of clericalism and 'old-worldliness.' But the *Rule of Benedict* prescribes, in fact, the opposite of that. Every monastery must of course include a priest; but his distinction lies only in his function, never in his status or privileges. And Abbatial government is not government by priests: we have no indication that even Benedict himself was ever ordained. The Rule was emphatically new-worldly, and retained its impetus to renewal and reformation, manifest, for instance, at Cluny and Clairvaux. What it amounted to was a new conception of monasticism, in which the community, not the hermit's solitude, was the ideal form; and by Benedictine witness and education, it inculcated a vision of society as community of faith, focused in the *Opus Dei*. That was the soul of Europe. That's the meaning of the cathedral at the heart of the city, and that's the meaning of the collegiate church at the heart of the university.

But it is a vision of community which still awaits fulfilment. In our own society, ecclesiastical and civil, we lack community of vocation and community of end. We have instead a plethora of vocations or ambitions, directed towards disparate and more or less private ends. May Benedict inspire us to seek a country – a community of praise. Nothing less than the *Opus Dei* will suffice; without that, all else is finally trivial and boring – a weariness of the flesh.

And what of Benedict's sanctity? We can do no better than to quote Gregory the Great, who says: 'The Reverend Father wrote a rule for monks, excelling in discretion, radiant and clear in its wording. If anyone desires to know intimately his character and life, all the manner of his work as Abbot is set forth in the precepts of this same Rule, for this holy man's teaching exactly followed his life.'

Amen.

ST BENEDICT AND ARCHBISHOP CRANMER

But they desire a better country, that is, an heavenly.

St Benedict was born in the year 480, or thereabouts – just fifty years after the death of Augustine; about a decade before the conversion of the Franks to Catholic Christianity; about a decade before the establishment of Theodoric's Ostrogothic kingdom in Italy. Those were turbulent times of transition, which would become still more turbulent later on when warring Gothic and Byzantine armies swept back and forth over Benedict's part of Italy. His great contemporaries, Boethius and Cassiodorus, responded with great insight, gathering together, translating and preserving the fragments that remained of a ruined and dying world. Benedict responded in a different way, by founding an institution which would become the major factor in the shaping of the new civilization of medieval Europe.

What we know of Benedict's life comes to us chiefly from Gregory the Great's *Dialogues*. Gregory tells us how the young Benedict came to Rome from Nursia – the modern Norcia, a rather obscure provincial town in a remote corner of Umbria, the 'Frigida Nursia' of Vergil's *Aeneid*. Gregory tells us how Benedict came to Rome to be educated in the liberal arts, and quickly went away again, shocked and disgusted by what seemed to him the moral vacuity of that life. He fled, says Gregory, '*scienter nescius, et sapienter indoctus*' (knowledgably ignorant and wisely unlearned).

Benedict's place of refuge is still to be seen – a cave in the mountainside high above Subiaco, the site of the ruined villa of the Emperor Nero: the ruins of the old and the birth-place of the new. The place was later adorned with medieval chapels; 'plastered like swallows' nests against the cliff', said Pius II; '*paradisi limen*', said Petrarch, 'the threshold of paradise.' After three years of solitude in that cave, Benedict emerged to establish monastic communities nearby. One of them still survives: Santa Scolastica, named in honour of Benedict's sister. Over its portal is inscribed the Benedictine motto, '*ora et labora*' (prayer and work) – the motto rather surprisingly borrowed by the pious Presbyterian founders of Dalhousie University.

Benedict's most important foundation was of course Monte Cassino, in 529, and it was there that he wrote his *Rule*, and it was from there that the Benedictine movement spread to cover the face of Europe, with hundreds upon hundreds of communities of Benedictine monks and nuns. With that movement we must associate so many of the great figures of early medieval Europe: Rhabanus Maurus in Fulde and Mainz, Anselm in Bec and Canterbury, Hildegard in Bingen on the Rhine, Gregory and Hildebrand in Rome, Bernard in Burgundy, Abélard in Normandy and Paris, and so on. And it is to that movement that we must attribute virtually everything that is great in early medieval art: the superb Romanesque architecture and sculpture of the Benedictine churches from northern Britain and Scandinavia to southern Italy and Sicily and Spain, the frescos and manuscript illuminations, the music of the liturgy, and so on. It was the Benedictine movement which more than any other force shaped and unified the civilization of early medieval Europe.

But, really, all that is incidental and beside the point. Benedict's *Rule* is not about building civilization in medieval Europe.

'They desire a better country.'

Benedict's *Rule* prescribes that nothing is to be preferred to the '*Opus Dei*' (the work of God), the work of prayer. The Benedictine life is built upon the *Opus Dei*, the day articulated by the canonical hours of prayer. Not prayer for the sake of anything else, but everything else for the sake of prayer; not prayer to inspire work, but work to support prayer; not prayer to motivate learning, but learning to inform prayer; not prayer to inspire the creation of beauty, but the creation of beauty to enhance prayer; not prayer for the sake of civilization, but civilization as a context for prayer. 'Let nothing be preferred to the *Opus Dei*.' 'They desire a better country', that is, a heavenly one.

It is simply a matter of historical coincidence that Archbishop Cranmer is commemorated along with St Benedict in our Church calendar. The archbishop was burnt at the stake on St Benedict's Day in 1556. There is, nevertheless, a remarkable appropriateness in the combination, for Cranmer's genius, and his enduring contribution to the Church's life, had to do precisely with the '*Opus Dei*', with the ordering of prayer. Basically, what Cranmer did in the *Book of Common Prayer* involved taking the canonical hours of the Benedictine tradition, conflating them into the two offices of Morning and Evening Prayer, providing them with Old Testament and New Testament lessons, and prescribing their daily use in all the cathedrals, collegiate churches and parish churches in the land. Thus the

Opus Dei was to become the daily work of all Christian people.

In effect, the nation becomes the monastery, the community articulated in prayer. In this, the vision of Cranmer was essentially a development of the Benedictine ideal, and it is an ideal which still awaits fulfilment. Nowadays, many Christians, including many liturgists, who really ought to know better, think of prayer as a kind of therapy for individuals or communities: prayer for the sake of personal efficiency or serenity; prayer for the sake of community self-consciousness – 'the gathering of the community', or whatever. Benedict and Cranmer both say 'No'. Not prayer for the sake of community, but community for the sake of prayer. The '*Opus Dei*' is not a means, but an end: for it is precisely our 'looking unto Jesus the author and finisher of our faith'.

Amen.

ST GREGORY THE GREAT

To you it is given to know the mysteries of the kingdom of Heaven.

St Gregory was bishop of Rome at the end of the sixth century – that profoundly ambiguous age: on the one hand, an age of widespread ruin and destruction, in which the ancient empire, long since overrun by marauding armies, seemed to have exhausted its last energies; on the other hand, an age in which the foundations of a new world were being laid, by a few Christians who, as Christopher Dawson remarks, 'had no idea of building up a new social order, but who laboured for the salvation of men in a dying world because time was short.'

Gregory was one of those foundation builders. As his successor put it, in an epitaph, 'In a straitened age, the Pope showed himself more generous, and disdained to be cast down, though the world failed.' What wonderful words! 'In a straitened age, he showed himself more generous, and disdained to be cast down, though the world failed.' Surely that is the stuff of sanctity! Gregory, amid the shipwreck of his world, was unperturbed, because he was, as the Venerable Bede says of him, 'fastened with the cable of an anchor to the peaceful shore of prayer.'

Gregory's pontificate was second to none in its influence upon the future form of Western Christianity. The English-speaking world, in particular, owes him an immeasurable debt, for it was he who remarkably discerned the English character of angels – '*Non Anglii, sed Angeli*', he said, 'not Angles, but angels'; and he sent Augustine to be their missionary, thus establishing the Church of Canterbury. And establishing much more than that, too, because that English Church became a great force for evangelizing Europe in the early Middle Ages, thereby helping to secure the foundations of the Holy Roman Empire. Thus Gregory's policies governed the shape of Europe for centuries to come.

And surely, we cannot forget the work of Gregory in codifying that form of sacred music called 'Gregorian', which became the standard form of Church music in medieval Europe, and has endured through all the following centuries. What precisely was Gregory's part in the development of Gregorian chant, we don't know; but we do know that he was very actively engaged in musical education. His biographer, John the Deacon, tells us that Gregory

> founded a school of singers [*orphanotrophium*], endowed it with some farms, and built for it two habitations, one under the steps of the basilica of St Peter the apostle, the other under the houses of the Lateran Palace. There to the present day [says John] are preserved the couch on which he used to recline while singing, and his whip with which he menaced the boys, together with his original antiphonary.

Gregory is celebrated as a doctor of the Church – one of the four great Latin doctors: Ambrose, Jerome, Augustine and Gregory – and he was greatly influential by his writings: by his commentaries on scripture, certainly, but above all, by his simple, very practical handbook on pastoral care, which was taken to Britain by St Augustine, and translated into West Saxon by King Alfred in the ninth century. Charlemagne made the study of it obligatory upon all the bishops in his empire, and it became customary to give a copy of it, together with the canons of the Church, into the hands of bishops at their consecration. Alcuin wrote to the archbishop of York in 796: ‘Wherever you go, let the pastoral book of St Gregory be your companion. Read and re-read it often that in it you may learn to know yourself and your work, that you may have before your eyes how you ought to live and teach.’

It is indeed, a wonderful little work, full of good sense, moderation and compassion. And undoubtedly the best book which has so far appeared in the field of pastoral theology. Let me give you just a very brief excerpt from it, to give you a taste of its character.

> When a preacher cries aloud in this time of darkness, he is as a cock crowing in the night, and says ‘It is now the hour for us to arise from sleep’ . . . The cock has the custom of crowing loud in the darkest hours of the night, but when morning is near, he reduces the length and volume of his notes. So, the true preacher proclaims aloud plain truths to hearts still in the dark, showing them no hidden mysteries. Then only are they to learn all the profounder things of Heaven, when they approach the light of truth.
>
> But at this juncture we are brought back in the zeal of our charity to what we have already said, namely, that every preacher should make himself heard rather by deeds than by words, and that by his righteous way of life should imprint footsteps for men to tread in . . . That cock, too . . . when he is preparing to crow, first shakes his wings, and beating himself with them, makes himself more alert.

> So, it is obviously necessary that they who give utterance to words of holy preaching, should first be awake in the earnest practice of good deeds, . . . Let them first rouse themselves up by lofty deeds, and then make others solicitous to live good lives. Let them first smite themselves with the wings of their thoughts . . . and discover in what respects they are idling and lagging, and make amends by severe penance. Then, and only then, let them set in order the lives of others by their words.

The gifts of grace in Gregory are gifts of clarity, of insight and disciplined steadiness of purpose, which will not be cast down, though the world fail. Those are gifts sorely needed in a troubled Church and in a troubled world, and in our own troubled lives. But they are gifts freely given by the Spirit to those who ask in faith, 'To you, it is given to know the mysteries. … Blessed are your eyes for they see, and your ears for they hear.' In a straitened age, may we, like St Gregory, become more generous, and disdain to be cut down though the world fail. May our Lenten disciplines help us to cultivate those gifts of grace, and express them in our lives, 'fastened with the cable of an anchor, to the peaceful shore of prayer'.

Amen.

ST JOHN OF DAMASCUS

Though he slay me, yet will I praise him.

Today we celebrate the festival of St John of Damascus, confessor and doctor of the Church. He is not, I think, one of the better-known saints, and perhaps I ought to begin by offering you something of a curriculum vitae.

He was born about 675 of a Christian family in Damascus, and succeeded his father as *logothete*, chief Christian representative, at the court of the Caliph. About 716 he was forced, on account of his faith, to give up his office, and withdrew to the monastery of St Sabas, near Jerusalem, where he became a priest.

He was a strong defender of images in the Iconoclastic controversy, and wrote several treatises on that subject; but no doubt his most important work was his great systematic treatise; the *Fountain of Knowledge*, in three parts, in which he discusses philosophy, heresy, and orthodox doctrine. The work could be regarded as a summation of the Greek Patristic tradition, and includes significant advances, especially in the doctrines of Trinity and Incarnation. All through the Middle Ages his works were used by the Greeks, and especially by the Slavs, and in the twelfth century a Latin translation of the third part of the *Fountain of Knowledge*, called *De Fide Orthodoxa* was used by Peter Lombard, and later by St Thomas Aquinas.

From these facts, it is clear that St John of Damascus was in the most obvious sense a doctor, a teacher, of the Church, though that fact was officially recognized by the Western Church only in 1890.

The sense in which he is a confessor is perhaps less clear, because the accounts we have of his troubles are somewhat confused, involving a forged letter, a charge of treason, a severed right hand miraculously restored, and so on. I don't think it would be very profitable for us, within the confines of this homily, to try to get to the bottom of this matter, so what more should I tell you?

If I were a properly relevant preacher, I suppose I could use this as an occasion to talk about Christian vocation, or Christian mission, in the upper echelons of the civil service, with John of Damascus as the exemplar; but I don't really want to do that. Rather, I want to say some simple things about what in general it means to be a confessor.

A confessor is one who confesses – who owns or acknowledges the faith in circumstances of persecution, or extreme risk; one who holds on to divine truth in contradiction to all worldly appearances; who gives thanks even from the bottom of the pit. 'Though he slay me', says Job, 'yet will I praise him.'

The witness of all the saints we celebrate through the Church's year constitutes a great spectrum of sanctity, in which the gifts of the spirit are manifest in all their marvellous diversity – 'dividing to everyone severally as he will'. And each of the saints manifests some essential aspect of this spectrum which is the wholeness or completeness of the spiritual kingdom, spread out for us through the cycle of the year, as Dante in the *Paradiso* has it spread out through all the spheres of the universe. Thus they continually recall us from the temptation to narrow our conceptions of sanctity, our temptation to see one-sidedly only this or that particular pattern as the only authentic Christian piety. In the graceful panorama of sanctity, confessors stand for that essential dimension of Christian spirituality which is the voice of praise – that voice of knowledge and love which gathers together our distracted experience, and articulates – confesses – its unity in its principle and end. The voice of praise is our return (and as St John of Damascus would have it, the return of all creation – for in the voice of praise 'earth itself confesses'). Against all worldly appearances, this voice must stand out – it is the fire of the spirit within us, bearing us aloft, which we dare not question. 'Yea though he slay me, yet will I praise him.'

I should like to apply to the confessor some words which Rilke applies to the poet:

> Tell us, Poet, what it is you do?
> I praise.
> But the deadly and monstrous things; how can you
> bear them, how can you accept them?
> I praise.
> But even what is nameless, what is anonymous,
> how can you call upon it?
> I praise.
> What right have you to be true in every disguise,
> beneath every mask?
> I praise
> And how is it that both calm and violent things,
> like star and storm, know you for their own?
> I praise.
>
> Only he who has raised the lyre even among the shades
> may sense and set forth the everlasting praise

Only he who has eaten of their poppy with the dead
    will never lose even the softest note.

This liturgy, in which we show forth the dying of the Son of God and our dying in him, is the medium and focus of our sacrifice of praise, and rightly do we call it a celebration.

Amen.

ST HENRY OF FINLAND

Land of Zebulon and land of Naphtali, by way of the sea, beyond Jordan, Galilee of the Gentiles; The people which sat in darkness have seen a great light; to them which sat in the region and shadow of death, light is arisen.

St Henry, styled by Johannes Magnus the 'Apostle and Patron of Finland', is not particularly well known in Anglican circles. In fact, until 1959, when he was added to the Canadian calendar, he seems to have been mostly of local interest in the Churches of Sweden, Finland, and Norway, where he was venerated from the Middle Ages onward, not as a missionary, as in our calendar, but as a martyr bishop. He has never been placed on the calendar of the Roman Catholic Church, although he is mentioned in Molanus's updated edition of the *Martyrology of Usuard*, upon which the modern Roman martyrology is based. We know that Henry was of English extraction, and that he was consecrated bishop of Uppsala, in Sweden, in 1152. He accompanied King St Eric of Sweden on his so-called 'crusade' against the pagan Finns in 1154, remaining in Finland as a missionary after Eric's victorious return home, and shortly afterward died a martyr's death, struck down by a Finnish soldier whom he had excommunicated as a murderer.

But it is as a missionary, and not as a martyr, that we are commemorating St Henry today, as a 'labourer in the Lord's harvest', a 'harvester of souls', a 'fisher of men'. That the Church views this office as primarily that of bishops, and by derivation of priests, is clear not only from today's collect, epistle, and gospel, but also from the fact that all but five of the missionaries commemorated in our calendar are bishops, the others, priests. Nevertheless, it is all too clear that unless the whole Church, clergy and laity, is healthy, then the Church's work of mission is bound to fail. Moreover, it is increasingly clear that to be a missionary today most often means never leaving one's own community. We all know that we do not live in a world in which the Church can simply take for granted that those who have been brought up in her will remain, or that those who worship within her now will continue to their lives' ends in her communion – nor should she! And so we see our Church constantly coming up with new ways of making churchgoing attractive. We hear of new 'models of the Church', we see an almost limitless proliferation of new and 'attractive' liturgies specifically tailored to every conceivable taste and concern. We try new and wonderful things in our parishes: coffee hours, study groups, groups for newlyweds, groups for singles. We have been the Church of the social gospel, the 'caring' Church, the 'progressive' Church, the 'inclusive' Church, whatever any of these tags mean. We will be anything, *anything* to make ourselves attractive, we will do anything to seem relevant. 'Let's fix the Church and everything else will follow.' 'If we build it, they will come.'

But what does our Lord say to this? What does he say to Martha at Bethany – Martha who bustles about, trying to get the house right, getting the food on the table, making everything perfect? Martha, whose sister, Mary – idle, listening to her guest's conversation – is not pulling her weight. 'Martha, Martha', he says, 'thou art careful and troubled about many things: But one thing is needful: and Mary hath chosen that good part, which shall not be taken away from her.'

He is speaking to us.

'One thing is needful.'

But what is that one thing?

The twentieth-century Anglican mystic Evelyn Underhill, in her 1936 address to the Worcester Diocesan Clergy Conference, gives us a clue. She is speaking specifically of priests, but her comments have a universal significance:

> … New machinery and, adaptations and adjustments, are not the first need of the Church …; but more devoted, adoring, sacrificial souls. These are supernatural qualities, given by God in our hours of direct attention to Him; and these are the only lasting sources of that charity, that invincible lovingkindness which will help us to *show the beauty of Christ to others and so win them for God*. It is terribly hard for human beings [to] believe this … but those who do carry it out have no doubt of its truth.

This is the one thing needful – to sit at the feet of Christ and listen to him. What can be attractive about the Church if not Christ himself and the triune God whose life he reveals? All of our running about patching holes, our tinkering with the Church's 'new machinery', our constant 'adjustments and adaptations', simply distract from that one thing needful. They draw us away from the true work of the Christian – work upon our own souls. It is there, you see, in our own hearts, that we come face to face both with ourselves and with our Lord. It is there that our Lord first confronts us – Galilee of the Gentiles, that land north of Jerusalem where God's people have been contaminated with the worship of the Gentile idols. That, you see, is first and foremost our own souls – it is in our own hearts that we worship the idols of our own devising, where we seek fulfilment in God's creatures rather than in God himself. It is to the Capernaum of our hearts that our Lord sends his Holy Spirit, saying: 'Repent; for the kingdom of heaven is at hand.' What else is the nagging of our conscience, if not that call to repentance that Christ's presence must compel, if only we were attentive enough to realize it for what it is? We must withdraw, at least for a time, within ourselves and there confront what we really are – the image of the triune God, disfigured by sin, our unity shattered by our seeking after the idols we have loved in place of him in whom alone our hearts can rest. But it is there also that we meet the very end of all our longings, that ground of all that we are, who alone can bring us peace. If by grace we seek him there, then he will surely enter the synagogue of our heart, and there both 'preach the Gospel of the kingdom, and heal all manner of sickness and all manner of disease' within *us*. We who have 'sat in darkness' shall see 'a great light.' There we shall behold 'the glory as of the only begotten of the Father, full of grace and truth.'

And what, finally, does this have to do with our vocation to mission? It is simply this, that it is only through this discipline that we will ever make the Church attractive. Can a 'caring' Church ever be anything apart from a Church in which we love one another as Christ has loved us? We would never speak of a 'caring family' except as meaning a family whose members cared for one another – to mean anything else by the phrase is mere abstraction. And so it is with the Church. As the image of the triune God is renewed in each Christian soul, that image becomes discernible to others. The person becomes a living image – an icon, in the Church's language – of Christ, the Incarnate Word. It is thus that the Church becomes beautiful, as her members, taught by God's Word written, nourished by his sacraments, seeking him in their hearts in repentance and cultivation of the virtues, become beautiful in imitation of their beautiful shepherd. That is our primary duty as missionaries.

We plead the holy sacrifices this day, as our collect says, that God will 'send forth many labourers into his harvest.' As we receive our Lord's most precious body and blood, let us ask for the grace to know and perform the one thing needful. I want to close this evening with the concluding words of St Gregory Nazianzen's *Oration on the Holy Lights*, which he preached on the Feast of the Epiphany in 381, and which expresses what I have been trying to say much better than my own words permit.

> Be purified, and you shall be clean (for God rejoices in nothing so much as in the amendment and salvation of man, on whose behalf is every discourse and every Sacrament), that you may be like lights in the world, a quickening force to all other men; that you may stand as perfect lights beside That great Light, and may learn the mystery of the illumination of Heaven, enlightened by the Trinity more purely and clearly, of Which even now you are receiving in a measure the One Ray from the One Godhead in Christ Jesus our Lord; to Whom be the glory and the might for ever and ever.
>
> Amen.

ST FRANCIS OF ASSISI

God forbid that I should glory, save in the cross of our Lord Jesus Christ, by whom the world is crucified unto me, and I unto the world.

If you were to visit the little town of Assisi, in the hills of Umbria, north of Rome, you would find there many vestiges of Francis, '*il poverello*', as he was called, 'the Little Poor Man' of Assisi. Greatest of those monuments, dominating the scene, is the great Gothic basilica, which began to rise within two years of Francis' death, and was soon to be richly adorned with the magnificent frescos by Cimabue and Giotto, which tell the story of St Francis.

To the modern mind, it seems, perhaps, paradoxical that the 'Little Poor Man' should be commemorated in all that rich triumph of Gothic art. And yet, we ought not, after all, to be surprised; for it was Francis, perhaps more than any other, who inspired that great evangelical renewal of Christian thought and life in thirteenth-century Italy, and beyond: that great revival of zeal for the gospel, which was to bear fruit in so many different forms, including the great scholastic summas of theology, the paintings of Giotto, and the poetry of Dante.

St Francis is not well-served by the popular iconography of modern times. We usually meet him as a statue perched upon a bird bath, or decorating a garden path; and we come away with impressions – according to our tastes – that he was perhaps a kind of thirteenth-century 'flower child', with all the innocent simplicity of Eden; perhaps a 'drop-out' from the grim formality of the medieval Church; or perhaps a primitive environmentalist of a rather sentimental sort. But those are wrong impressions. St Francis was not a sentimentalist, but a severe and dedicated reformer, whose deepest hope was to shore up the crumbling foundations of the Church, by recalling it to its evangelical vocation.

St Francis and the brothers he assembled around him were not monks, living in monasteries in the old way, 'far from the places where men dwell' (as the charter of the Cistercian Order, for instance, had expressed it); they were friars, who went begging for their living, and their houses were simply the headquarters of itinerant preachers, who went out into the streets of the burgeoning new commercial towns and cities, preaching at the market crosses. They were the great missionaries of their time, a great new instrument of evangelism in that new bourgeois society, stemming the tide of secularism in Europe, and venturing forth even to evangelise the Muslims. St Francis himself preached before the Sultan of Morocco (without notable success, I'm afraid), and his missionaries penetrated far into Asia, even as far as India and China – a remarkable achievement in the thirteenth century. It was a vast missionary enterprise.

But what was the essence of that Franciscan mission? I think it could perhaps be summed up, rather paradoxically, as an other-worldly worldliness. It was a zealous service in the world for other-worldly reasons and other-worldly ends. It was a piety which could be freely active in the world, precisely because it was liberated from the world, freed from narrow, worldly, vested interests, by the cross of Jesus Christ, 'by which', as St Paul puts it, 'the world is crucified to me, and I unto the world.'

Much has been made, for instance, of St Francis' special

affinity to nature, and we all know about his preaching to the birds, even if we might be a little vague about the content of the sermon. But his relation to nature was not sentimental, nor aesthetic, nor utilitarian, but rather, deeply evangelical and theological. Nature is creation: creation, 'groaning in travail together until now, waiting for redemption'; creation waiting 'to be set free from its bondage to corruption', from the vanity of narrow, worldly ends; creation, waiting 'with eager longing for the revealing of the sons of God.'

Thus St Francis was missionary to the whole creation, preaching to the sun, and moon, and stars, to all the elements of earth, and fire, and air, and water, to all the animals, and all the fruits and flowers, and to all mankind. He would have the whole creation delivered from 'corruption', from worldly, fleshly, deathly ends, to find its meaning and its destiny in a symphony of praise. That is the meaning of his great 'Canticle of the Sun', which is paraphrased in one of our hymns:

> All creatures of our God and King,
> Lift up your voice and with us sing
> Alleluia, Alleluia!
> Thou burning sun with golden beam,
> Thou silver moon with softer gleam:
> O praise him, O praise him,
> Alleluia, Alleluia, Alleluia.

It is a spiritual vision which can be content with nothing less than raising up the life of earth, in all its fullness, to the fuller life of heaven. And the cross of Christ is at the heart of that vision, because it is the cross which shatters and puts an end to our narrow worldliness, and cancels our bondage to every worldly, fleshly vanity: 'The world is crucified unto me, and I unto the world.' That preaching of the cross was the mission of St Francis, and that mission found a miraculous seal in his own person, when, two years before his death, he received the 'stigmata' – 'the marks of the Lord Jesus'; the signs, in his own body, of the wounds of Jesus crucified. The glory of St Francis is the glory of the cross.

Now, if one dare suggest that we might still have lessons to learn from the medieval Church, perhaps one such lesson is here, in the witness of St Francis. The Church's life today is troubled by what is thought to be a tension between those who would be devoutly other-worldly, and those who would be zealous, up-to-date activists, busy doing good in the world. The witness of St Francis is that that opposition is a false one; that, in fact, other-worldly detachment, the cancelling of worldliness through the cross of Jesus Christ, is actually the liberation of the springs of action, and the very starting point and basis of genuinely Christian service in this world. Without that, our service turns out to be little more than 'bondage to corruption' and pursuit of worldly vanities, which yield a bitter harvest.

'But God forbid that I should glory, save in the cross of our Lord Jesus Christ, by which the world is crucified to me, and I unto the world.'

Amen.

ST THOMAS AQUINAS, FIRST SERMON

In the day of visitation they will shine out as doth the sun; And run to and fro as sparks among the stubble.

Those of you who are familiar with the symbolic astronomy of Paradise, as it is set out in Dante's *Divine Comedy*, will recall that in the heaven of the sun, the doctors of the Church form garlands of light, gyrating in celestial dances, uttering a music of such ineffable sweetness that it cannot be described on earth. They symbolize the order and harmony in which all the push and pull, all the balances and counterbalances, all of the divine manifestations of God's truth, are in paradise conjoined and reconciled.

'They shine out as doth the sun. They run to and fro as sparks among the stubble.' And in this heaven of the sun – this realm of intellectual illumination (for that is what the image stands for), Dante's first spokesman is St Thomas, whose festival we celebrate today, and whose merit we venerate.

But for most of us, I think, the celebration and veneration of the saints are not easy matters. We cannot rejoice without explanation, we cannot venerate without apology. We do not easily see our doctors as garlands of light. Aware as we are of the manifold factors, social, political, economic, and so on, which condition and limit each person's life, and astute as we are in suspecting the labyrinth of dubious motivations underlying each ostensibly good action, it seems that our rejoicing must be always rather tentative, our veneration somehow qualified.

The saints, whether medieval scholastics, or modern martyrs in Uganda, were, after all men and women like ourselves, with all sorts of peculiarities and eccentricities, and complicated psyches, and limited understanding. They all pursued, no doubt, some particular good, as they saw it – even those who spent much of their lives perched on pillars in the desert. But can we venerate this morass of human preference and particularity? Surely there is none good save God alone!

But what we celebrate in the festival of the saints is precisely the goodness of God in the triumphs of his grace; and what we venerate is the manifestation of his glory. And, as the Word was made flesh in all the particularity of Bethlehem, and Nazareth, and Calvary, so the grace of God triumphs not in the idea, but in the actual particularities and eccentricities of human lives, and manifests itself always in the pursuit and attainment of some particular good.

In this the saint is like the tragic hero, and it was not without reason that the early Christians saw in the Greek heroes the images of saints and even of Christ himself. Many works of early Christian art quite boldly make that scandalous conflation. But the tragic flaw, the *hubris* of the hero, lies in the pride which fastens upon the particular, the partial good, as though it were the whole; the gracious merit of the saint lies in the humility of faith which sees the part as only a part.

The heaven of the sun is the realm of intellectual illumination, and St Thomas is its first spokesman, for he, in extraordinary degree, stands for the pursuit of the good of intellect. Therefore his festival is of special interest in an academic community. 'The study of philosophy', says Thomas to Siger of Brabant, 'does not mean to learn what others have thought, but to learn what is the truth of things.' Not that we should aspire to become Thomists – though I suppose we could do much worse, and I could suggest some possibilities – but rather that we should see in Thomas the pattern of the pursuit of that particular good which belongs to us as scholars. Thomas is not a saint just because he pursued the good of the theoretical sciences with an integrity, and intensity, and a clarity hardly equalled; but because in him that pursuit was encompassed by a humility which could see his stupendous achievement as only a part, indeed as straw, in comparison with faith's vision of Truth which is God.

On the feast of St Nicholas, in the year 1273, according to the acts of his canonization, Thomas put down his pen, and laid aside the uncompleted *Summa Theologica*, and all through that last winter of his life, he wrote no more. 'I can write no more', he said. 'All that I have hereto written seems to me nothing but straw.'

Dante, I think, captures the spirit of that conclusion, when, in the end of Canto X of the *Paradiso*, he has Thomas introduce Siger of Brabant, the Averroist, Thomas' most notorious opponent – now a light, at Thomas' side, in the circle of the doctors:

> That's the eternal light of Siger, who
> lecturing down in Straw Street, hammered home
> Invidious truths, as logic taught him to.

Amen.

ST THOMAS AQUINAS, SECOND SERMON

The true beginning of wisdom is the desire of discipline, and the care of discipline is love; and love is the keeping of her laws . . . therefore the desire of discipline bringeth to a kingdom.

When we think about the thirteenth century, it may be that we still labour under a certain nineteenth-century distortion of perspective, according to which that greatest of medieval centuries is still described as the 'Age of Faith' or the 'Age of the Great Medieval Synthesis', in contrast to what Matthew Arnold once described as 'this strange disease of modern life, with its sick hurry, its divided aims'. That there is an element of truth in the Romantic view is surely impressed upon anyone who thoughtfully regards the great Gothic churches of that time, or considers the great scholastic *summas* of philosophy and theology. But, in fact, those great monuments of faith and scholarship arose in a century of revolutionary turbulence, social and political, aesthetic and religious and intellectual, and most of those monuments are actually strong witness to that turbulence.

You must not think of Thomas as living out his days in the cloistral calm of some Benedictine or Cistercian house, 'far from the place where men dwell', as the old Cistercian charter puts it. Though he began his education in St Benedict's own monastery of Monte Cassino, he was very soon won, against the violent opposition of his family, to the new order of Dominicans, itinerant, mendicant preachers in the busy world of burgeoning cities and universities.

No *stabilitas* of place for Thomas; think of him rather, as trudging across the face of Europe, always on foot, as befitted a mendicant, first from Monte Cassino to the new university of Naples, then to Paris (a long walk across the Alps), and on to Cologne to study with Albertus Magnus, back again to Paris to become *Baccalaureus* and *Magister*, then called to the papal court to lecture, at Agnani, Orvieto, Rome and Viterbo, then back to Paris to face the Averroist controversy, back again to Naples, always lecturing or preaching or writing expert opinions on one controversy or another, and finally a winter journey in 1273-74 to the Council of Lyons, interrupted at the Benedictine house at Fossanova, where he died at the age of forty-nine.

No *stabilitas* of place; nor were these times of intellectual *stabilitas*. To most of Thomas's contemporaries, the study of the works of Aristotle and the Arabic commentators was still a risky business, and a dire threat to the Christian faith, and the prohibition of several of the major works of Aristotle was renewed at Paris as late as 1263 by Pope Urban IV. But despite such prohibitions, by the middle of the thirteenth century the intellectual frontiers were, in fact, wide open, and the sudden mingling of strange new strains of learning resulted in vigorous conflict and controversy between Franciscans, Dominicans, and Averroists. Thomas was at the storm-centre of those controversies, and some of his propositions were actually condemned in 1277. Thomas seems to have been afraid of nothing – except (we are told) thunderstorms.

In view of all the turbulent circumstances, and the busyness of his life, one can hardly fail to be astonished by the serene discipline of Thomas. Not only the sheer quantity of precise and careful work (nearly one hundred treatises which fill about thirty large volumes), but even more perhaps by the calm lucidity of even the most controversial works, with never a violent exclamation, and never a trace of an argument *ad hominem*. What is the secret of this nearly incomprehensible achievement?

In the end, nothing will explain it but the true sanctity of Thomas, the discipline of love, the mind's steady focus, the mind in love with God. 'These three things concur', says Thomas, 'vision, which is the perfect knowledge of the intelligible end; comprehension, which is the presence of that end; and delight or enjoyment, which is the ease of lover with beloved'.

> Not merely gathering information about divine things, but also submitting one's self to them, this is not only a matter of information, but also of falling in love with the things of God, and cleaving to them by affection . . . Things understood are in the mind in the mind's own fashion, but desire goes out to things as they are in themselves; love would transform us into the very condition of their being.

Thomas' sanctity is that of the mind in love with God and formed by the discipline of love. 'The true beginning of wisdom is the desire of discipline, and the care of discipline is love.' It seems singularly appropriate that Thomas in the last months of his life at Fossanova, put aside his great *summa* of theology, incomplete, and gave his last efforts to explaining to the monks the Song of Solomon, that mystical love song of bridegroom and bride, of God and the soul, of Christ and the Church. As one of his earliest biographers tells us, '*ut cantando moreretur et moriendo cantaret* – so that by singing he might die, and by dying he might sing, he was caught up to heaven, more by the power of love than by the power of death.'

His epitaph might be from the Song of Solomon:

> With great delight I sat in his shadow and his fruit was sweet to my taste. He brought me to the banqueting house and his banner over me was love.

Amen.

ALL SAINTS

There is one body, and one Spirit, even as ye are called in one hope of your calling ... But unto every one is given grace according to the measure of the gift of Christ.

In the collect for All Saints' Day, we pray that God's grace may enable us to follow the blessed saints in all virtuous and godly living; and I think we might do well to consider on this festival just why we need the example of the saints, and how we should go about imitating them.

In general of course the importance of examples is obvious enough, and I'm sure that each of us must recognize in his own life the importance of examples of one sort or another: the examples of our parents, of our teachers, of our pastors, of our friends and neighbours, the examples of those we have most admired in public and in private life. The power of example, for good or ill, is surely fundamental in our growing up, in the shaping of our lives at every stage, and we are the sort of characters we are very largely because of the examples we have admired and imitated.

But why the example of the saints? In Christian life, after all, the one example, perfect and complete, is Jesus Christ himself, the very Son of God, the beginning and the end, the author and finisher of faith. Surely Christ himself must be the one object of our imitation, and the pattern of our lives. What need have we of any other? On just such grounds as these, many of our fellow-Christians, in the Reformation and in more recent times, have abolished the festivals of saints. And we ourselves, although we have held on to the festivals, are inclined to give them rather perfunctory attention.

But it is a mistake to oppose the example of our Saviour Christ to the example of his saints, as though they were alternatives. The example of the saints is nothing other than the following of Christ: they are examples of the following of Christ, in different times and places, in various callings and different circumstances. The following of Christ is not just one kind of life. As St Paul expresses it, in his wonderful discussion of the diversity of gifts, in 1 Corinthians 12, 'Are all apostles? Are all prophets? Are all teachers? Are all workers of miracles?' – and so on. The Christian life is the life of a spiritual community, in which there are many different gifts and many different callings. St Paul compares it to a body, in which each member has its special place and function: 'And the eye cannot say unto the hand, I have no need of thee: nor again the head to the feet, I have no need of you.' 'Now ye are the body of Christ', he says, 'and members in particular.'

There are many different gifts, and many different callings, and therefore many different ways of imitating Christ. There is certainly something common to all genuinely Christian forms of life, and today's gospel lesson expresses that superbly in the Beatitudes of Jesus: we must all hunger and thirst for righteousness, we must all strive for that purity of heart which prepares us to see God. But there is also diversity, and even individuality, in the imitation of Christ, and it is of great practical importance to our own spiritual lives that we understand that. Sanctity is one thing, but its forms are manifold, and each one of us must find the form which suits his own God-given gifts and calling.

The calendar of saints sets before us that diversity in the following of Christ, and patterns of different forms of Christian life. Not all of us should be hermits in the desert like St Anthony, though we must all sometimes undertake lonely struggles of the soul. Not all of us should be contemplative monks or nuns, though all of us must share somehow in that life of pure prayer and adoration. Not all of us should be teachers, or doctors, or priests, or politicians, or butchers, or bakers, or candlestick makers, though some of us should be. Not all of us should be husbands, or wives, or fathers, or mothers, though perhaps most of us should be; and so on. There is diversity of gifts and diversity of callings.

The saints represent that diversity. But even so, it may well be that the example of no one saint is precisely right for you or me. For instance, St Mary is the greatest of all the saints, and for Christian mothers she seems the pattern to be imitated; and sometimes people look to the holy family of Nazareth as the pattern of Christian family life. Well, no doubt the greatest virtues shine forth there as nowhere else; but yet, that life cannot be precisely ours. St Mary's vocation as bearer of the Word of God and St Joseph's calling as protector of that Word are, after all, very peculiar, very special callings. We are all in some sense bearers and protectors of the Word of God, but not in the same sense as they were, and none of us has exactly their vocation. There is much there to be imitated, but also much which is beyond our imitation. Some mothers would certainly find a closer example in St Monica, who was a good wife to a pagan husband who came to share her faith only late in life, and mother of an exceedingly wayward son, Augustine, who eventually became the greatest saint of Latin Christendom. Monica's vocation seemed to have involved many tears; but as

Bishop Ambrose advised her, it was impossible that the son of such tears as hers should be lost.

I might continue with endless examples of one kind and another, but my point is this: our following of Christ means different things, many different gifts and many different callings, many different struggles and many different forms of sanctity in the community of faith; many different saints, some very close to us, and some remote, 'a multitude which no man could number, of all nations and kindreds and peoples and tongues', a thousand different tribulations, and a thousand different triumphs.

In this Festival of All Saints, we rejoice in that diversity, and we enlarge our vision to look upon and venerate God's gifts and graces in all that manifold expression, knowing that behind it all, there is one faith, one hope, one all-embracing charity, one 'growing up', as St Paul says, 'into Christ, who is the head … from whom the whole body, fitly joined together, and compacted by that which every joint supplieth, according to the effectual working in the measure of every part, maketh increase of the body to the building up of that body in love'.

Amen.

ALL SAINTS/ALL SOULS

Blessed are the pure in heart, for they shall see God.

In the lesson for today, from the Book of Revelation, St John the Divine, the seer of Patmos, sets before us his vision of the glory of the saints in heaven: 'a great multitude, which no one could number, of all nations, and kindreds, and people and tongues … clothed in white robes, and palms in their hands.' A great multitude, rapt in the everlasting praise of God. Delivered from trial and tribulation, 'they shall hunger no more, neither thirst any more, neither shall the sun light on them, nor any heat. For the Lamb which is in the midst of the throne shall feed them, and shall lead them unto living fountains of waters: and God shall wipe away all tears from their eyes'.

It is a vision which has moved Christian thought and aspiration all down the centuries; a vision remembered and re-echoed and expressed in liturgy and poetry, in painting and sculpture and architecture and music. Couldn't you just taste the longing for the heavenly Jerusalem in that final composition by Johann Sebastian Bach which was today's organ prelude: 'Before thy throne I now appear.' The vision of the holy city, God's new Jerusalem, and the glory of the blessed saints, has caught the imagination and illumined the path of countless weary travellers, foot-sore and weighed down by all the pains and troubles of their pilgrimage.

Lift your eyes, ye sons of light,
Sion's city is in sight;
There our endless home shall be,
There our Lord we soon shall see.

But for many modern Christians, I'm afraid that such a vision seems highly problematical. Heaven and the glory of the saints seem remote considerations, and quite irrelevant to the living of our lives, quite irrelevant to the pressing and all-consuming problems of our families, our familiar occupations, and the manifold troubles of the world in which we live. There is just no time for heaven. And so we would banish heaven to the realm of dreams and wishful thinking, and get on with the business of our lives here and now.

Heaven seems impossibly remote; and so we try to live our lives constricted by the narrow bounds of worldly ends, in pettiness and boredom, and frantic greeds for worldly satisfactions, which, however refined and elevated, can never really satisfy. The loss of heaven does not enhance our earthly lot, but, rather, condemns it to frustration and despair. It is that festering hopelessness which is the nursery of violence and malice and a thousand kinds of nastiness. And it's a hopelessness so deep that no amount of bread and circuses can ever touch it. It is a sad, sad business, after all, to be dissatisfied with earth and to have no lively hope of heaven. To give up heaven is to settle for hell – an eternity of frustrated longing.

The longing for heaven – 'heavenly avarice', as Traherne calls it – however inarticulate or ill-defined, is endemic to our very nature. Dante makes the point beautifully in his *Convivio*:

Therefore, I say, that not only in the gaining of knowledge

and wealth, but in any acquisition whatsoever, human desire extends itself, in one way and another. And the reason is this: the deepest desire of each thing, arising from its very nature, is to return to its principle [source]. And because God is the principle [source] of our soul, and has made it like himself (as it is written, 'Let us make man in our image and likeness'), the soul mightily desires to turn to him.

And so, as a pilgrim (*peregrino*) who travels along a road he has not been on before, believes each building, seen in the distance, is the inn, and finding it not so, directs his belief to the next, and so from house to house, until at last he finds the inn; just so our soul, as soon as it enters upon the new and unfamiliar road of this life, directs its eyes towards the end, the highest good, and each thing it sees which manifests some good, it takes to be that end.

And because its knowledge is at first imperfect, inexperienced and untaught, little goods seem great to it, and thus it begins its longing first with them. Thus we see infants intensely longing for an apple; and then, later on, for a little bird; and then, still further on, fine clothes; and then a horse; and then a mistress; then, modest riches; then more; and then still more. And that is because in none of these things does it find that for which it ever seeks, and it believes to find it further on …

Indeed, we may lose the road by error, just as we may lose our way on earthly roads. Just as there is from one city to another one best and straightest road, and another which diverts us altogether (going in the opposite direction), and many others which divert us more or less; so in human life there are diverse roads, of which one is the most true, another most false, and others more or less true or

> false. And just as we see that the straightest road goes to the city, fulfills our longing, and gives rest from toil, and that the road which goes the opposite way never achieves that end; so it is in our life, that the good wayfarer (*lo bono camminatore*) reaches the goal and has rest, while he who goes astray never reaches it, but with great agony of soul ever gazes onward with greedy eyes.

This commemoration of All Saints and All Souls sets before our eyes a vision which is no vague and empty dream, no figment of the imagination, but a way of life – 'a best and straightest road' – a prescription as practical and relevant as any can ever be. That prescription is spelled out in the gospel for today: 'Blessed are the poor in spirit' – blessed are those who know their own spiritual poverty – 'theirs is the kingdom of heaven. Blessed are they that mourn, for they shall be comforted'. 'Blessed are the meek' – the gentle – 'for they shall inherit the earth' – they are the heirs of God's promises. 'Blessed are they which do hunger and thirst after righteousness, for they shall be filled. Blessed are the merciful, for they shall obtain mercy. Blessed are the pure in heart, for they shall see God. Blessed are the peace-makers, for they shall be called the children of God. Blessed are they which are persecuted for righteousness' sake, for theirs is the kingdom of heaven.' What is it, after all, that separates us from the glory of the saints? What is it but our pride, our hardness of heart, our vainglory, our self-seeking, our hypocrisy? By the fire of God's grace all that must be done away. No doubt, it is only through pains and troubles, only through great tribulations, that the dross of mind and heart will be purged. And therefore, we must embrace our tribulations, as the Gospel bids us: 'Rejoice and be exceeding glad, for great is your reward in heaven.'

Our pains and troubles are not obstacles, our circumstances are not obstacles; the real obstacles are nothing but aspects of ourselves – our pride, our complacency, our stubborn and narrow preoccupation with worldly ends. By the grace of God, all that must be put away. As St Peter expresses it, 'Laying aside all malice, and all guile, and hypocrisies, and envies, and all evil-speakings, as newborn babes, desire the sincere milk of the word, that ye may grow thereby.'

God's kingdom is within our grasp: but only if that is what we want and seek above all else, and with all our heart. That is what purity of heart means – that singleness of purpose which wills one thing, entirely and totally; which, like the merchant of Jesus' parable, is ready to sell all that he has to buy one precious pearl. 'Blessed are the pure in heart, for they shall see God.'

We join today in a festival of hope and expectation. May the grace of God, in the example, and the fellowship, and the fervent prayers of the community of the saints, support us, uplift us, and strengthen our own feeble steps. As Peter Abelard puts it, in his Sabbath evening hymn:

> Now in the meantime, with hearts raised on high,
> We for that country must yearn and must sigh;
> Seeking Jerusalem, dear native land,
> Through our long exile on Babylon's strand.

Amen.

ALL SOULS

Work out your own salvation with fear and trembling. For it is God which worketh in you, both to will and to do of his good pleasure.

November is a month of contrast – the final battle-ground of summer and winter. The garden still produces a few late flowers which have long withstood attacks of frost; but one knows that any morning now one might wake up to find them buried under snow. One reconciles oneself to the fact that, for a few months at least, winter is going to win. But one plants a few crocus bulbs in token of one's faith that March will surely come.

The calendar of the Christian year follows closely the rhythm of nature's cycle, and for that calendar, too, November is a month of contrast. It is ushered in with the Festival of All Saints, the glorious final harvest of the Spirit, when all the fragments are gathered up in a celebration of joy, and peace and life fulfilled. It is a glorious festival, all white and gold. But then, the very next day, the livery of God's servants is changed to black for the observance of All Souls, and mass is said for all the faithful souls departed. And the tone of the ancient mass of requiem is certainly far from cheerful: '*Dies irae, dies illa*' – 'Day of wrath and doom impending/David's word with Sibyl's blending/Heaven and earth in ashes ending.' It seems a very grim business; and what a contrast with All Saints: all the difference between life and death.

In older, and perhaps more reasonably pious times than ours,

November was sometimes called the Month of the Dead and the Church's ordo for that month bristled with requiem masses. Nowadays, freed of all morbid superstition, we recognize that Christians are 'Resurrection People' and that all are therefore saints. With All Saints thus 'democratized', why bother about All Souls?

But meanwhile, we seem to have forgotten what death is all about, and what Christians do about it; and so the ordo bristles now, instead, with lots of little conferences on 'death and dying' and there's a great spate of little 'bookies' on the subject. Of course, such efforts are not to be disparaged; but do you suppose one might be forgiven the heretical thought that the requiem masses were really more to the point – intellectually, morally, and (dare one add) aesthetically? Talking things over has its place, but there are also things to be done. In this case, the thing to be done is prayer.

Well, anyway, here we are in the middle of an old-fashioned mass of requiem, and we should consider what it means. As I've already suggested, the texts of the mass are not particularly cheerful. They imply that we are not quite all saints, and that getting to be saints is a painful and difficult business, a long and narrow road, with judgement at the end.

Sanctity is a problem. As we learned from the All Saints gospel lesson, it means 'purity of heart', that is to say, to be a saint is to will in all things only the pure and simple and perfect good, which is God: to love God with all the heart, and all the soul, and all the mind, and all the strength, and in the perspective of that love, to love one's neighbour as oneself. That is purity of heart: to will one thing – only the pure and simple and perfect good. 'Blessed are the pure in heart, for they shall see God.' Blessed are those whose loves are all united in the one love of God.

But who, then, is 'pure of heart'? Our wills are certainly

not simple. We will so many things, so many 'goods', so many 'bads', and we get so confused about them, and, as St Paul says, even the good that we would do, we do not, and the evil that we would not do, that is precisely what we do. 'If thou, Lord, wilt be extreme to mark what is done amiss, O Lord, who may abide it?' Our goodness is very limited, and so remarkably fragile that we work out our salvation 'in fear and trembling.'

Our good works will never save us: the most and best that can be said for us is that finally, by God's grace, we really intend the good; and we must trust to God, who gives us that, to make it perfect. When we speak of the 'faithful' departed, we speak of those whose final choice, even if only in the last moment of all life's choosings, was for the good, and we trust to God to make that perfect – to purify the heart.

We pray for the departed, as we pray for one another here and now. We do not cease to be our brother's keepers when we commend them to God's keeping, and we plead Christ's sacrifice for them and us. The prayer is essentially the same: that God, who works in them and us, both to will and to do his good pleasure, may make perfect that work in all of us; that we come finally to the peace of the saints, the purity of heart which wills one thing.

The life of the soul is not just summery bliss – not just the vision of the glory of all the saints – it is also the winter of struggle in the dark, and life goes down, even into death. But as in nature, so in grace, there is a providential care, and the seed which falls to the earth and dies can rise again and have its bloom in God's eternal spring. 'Fear and trembling', yes; but 'it is God that worketh in us'. And, therefore, as the lovely Russian *Kontakion of the Departed* expresses it, 'Weeping o'er the grave, we make our song – Alleluia, alleluia, alleluia.'

Amen.

INSTITUTIONAL LIFE: SACRED AND SECULAR

HARVEST FESTIVAL

For as the rain cometh down, and the snow from heaven, and returneth not thither, but watereth the earth, and maketh it bring forth and bud, that it may give seed to the sower, and bread to the eater: So shall my word be that goeth forth out of my mouth; it shall not return unto me void, but it shall accomplish that which I please, and it shall prosper in the thing whereto I sent it.

The Harvest Season is undoubtedly a time of great beauty, but I think that for many people it is rather a sad and depressing time, when the cycle of nature seems to come to an end in decay and death; and the gold and vermilion rhapsody of field and woodland seem to be merely the swansong of a dying beauty. The trees now clad in glory will soon become what the Bard describes as 'Bare ruined choirs, where late the sweet birds sang.' The days shorten and the light dies.

But to celebrate a festival of harvest is surely not to celebrate decay and death. Rather, it involves seeing in the cycle of nature something moving to fulfilment and completion. What we celebrate is not something lost, but something gained, something for which the seed-time, and the months of nourishment and growth have all been a preparation, a preamble. From that standpoint, the glory of this season is not a swansong of dying beauty, but praise and thanksgiving for something that has come to fruition.

We have prayed that our daily bread might be given, and today we give thanks that in the order of nature that petition has been richly granted us. For that, it surely behooves us to be grateful, and surely, too, in a world where so many are without bread, it behooves us to mix our gratitude with compassion and responsibility.

That is an important and serious matter, and that is what our Harvest Festival is about. But it is about something else, too, and something even more important. The lessons appointed for this occasion remind us of a further and deeper dimension of the Festival.

'As the rain cometh down … So shall my word be that goeth forth …'

In the course of nature – in its cycle of seed-time and harvest – there is a parallel to the course of human life and human history, and a parallel between that bread which sustains our bodily life, and that heavenly bread, the Word of God, which nourishes the human spirit. Thus the festival of daily bread and the harvest of the earth is also, more profoundly, a festival of the Word of God and the harvest of human souls.

Just as, for some, the conclusion of nature's cycle is a time of sadness and regret, so too, for some, is the cycle of human life and human history essentially a pretty sad and regretful business: we eat and drink and are relatively satisfied; we buy and sell and consume; we are educated and entertained and make progress – or at least we keep on going. We struggle to hold on to youth and fend off the ravages of the years; but we know that sooner or later it will certainly all be over, and what does it all come to in the end? 'Eat, drink, and be merry', urges the cynic, but the merriment perhaps wears a little thin.

This Harvest Festival points us to an altogether different

view of human life, a view according to which the course of our life moves towards a completion which is not decay but a fruition. 'The seed is the word of God', says Jesus in the parable of the sower, and the course of our life is nothing other than the bringing of that fruit to perfection. Our care and our concern is the nutriment, and cultivation and maturation of the human soul. And to that end, every word and every deed has, for better or worse, its effects upon ourselves and others.

The scriptures for this Festival urge us to consider this matter with the greatest earnestness.

In the Epistle: 'Wherefore do ye spend money for that which is not bread? And your labour for that which satisfieth not? Hearken diligently unto me, and eat ye that which is good, and let your soul delight itself in fatness. Incline your ear, and come unto me: hear, and your soul shall live'.

In the Gospel: 'Jesus said, "Labour not for the meat which perisheth, but for that meat which endureth unto everlasting life, which the Son of Man shall give unto you:… for the bread of God is he which cometh down from heaven, and giveth life unto the world".'

It seems to me that we engage ourselves mightily in pursuit of the meat that perisheth, and, like the ancient Israelites in the wilderness trying to amass treasuries of manna, we find to our dismay that it melts away and vanishes. Like the prosperous farmer in the Gospel, we would tear down our barns and build greater: 'Thou fool, this night thy soul will be required of thee', and 'What shall it profit anyone, if he shall gain the whole world, and lose his own soul?'

Our life is between seed-time and harvest, and for each of us, and all of us, the time of harvest must come. Let us concern ourselves then with the nutriment and maturation of our souls.

In this Harvest Festival, let us give thanks for our daily bread. But let us also give thanks for that true bread which cometh down from heaven to nourish and enlighten our souls.

Let us give thanks for the harvest of the earth. But let us also give thanks for that harvest of the Word of God, that harvest of human souls, which is the communion of those souls brought to fruition in the knowledge and love of God.

God's Word has gone forth into the world, and it will not return to him void, but it will accomplish that harvest which is his will.

Amen.

MARRIAGE, FIRST SERMON

This do, and thou shalt live.

Weddings are generally highly romantic and sentimental occasions, and no doubt that is a good thing. At least it is a good thing that in a world which seemed to have become in so many ways rather drab and prosaic we should still be able, sometimes, to celebrate the beauty of romance and rejoice in an occasion of human sentiment. That surely is a good thing.

But it is a good thing also that we have the liturgy of the Church and the lessons of the Scripture to remind us that what we celebrate here is also something more than natural sentiment and romantic engagement. Those feelings may indeed have their place in the marriage bond but they are not, after all, what is essential to it. They are not its basis. What is fundamental is the vow of mutual love, and the marriage service makes that point abundantly clear. And the vow, you know, is not a matter of sentiment or of transitory emotions. A vow is a matter of rational perception and steadfast will.

One cannot vow eternal affection. Our affections come and go; they wax and wane. But one can vow eternal love, and that is what is essential to the sacrament of matrimony, the vow of mutual love.

Now love is a much-used word and no doubt also a much-abused word. We often use it to refer to our natural affections and preferences, and so on. But those natural affections and preferences are not really love, though they may be the accoutrements of love. Sometimes they help and support love and that is a happy circumstance when that is so. But sometimes also they get in the way of love and obstruct it and distort it, and sometimes love itself requires that our affections and desires be verily crucified. As the Epistle puts it in this service,

'They that are Christ's have crucified the flesh with the affections and lusts.'

No, love is not affection or sentiment; it is not a matter of warm and friendly feelings inside. It is a matter of reason and will. To love one another in the sense in which we are commanded to love is to perceive and will the eternal good of one another and to act in terms of that will. To will the eternal good of one another whether we feel like it or not. That is the straight gate; that is the narrow road that leads to life. 'This do and thou shalt live', says Jesus to the lawyer in our Gospel lesson. This vow of love, this vow to will the eternal good of one another, is the vow to which all Christians are committed. It is implicit in the vows of baptism. And the vows of matrimony, like the vows of ordination and the vows of monastic life and so on, simply make those baptismal vows specific and concrete with respect to one permanent particular relationship.

'This do and thou shalt live', says Jesus. But how are we to do this? Our own needs, our own fears, our own affections and preferences and prejudices keep getting in the way of it. So needful ourselves, we can hardly see another's good and will it. We pass by on the other side. So preoccupied in ourselves we can hardly receive or accept another's good will towards us, and we begin to make excuse. We are really not very good perhaps, at love.

But fortunately our love is not the starting point. The starting point is God's love for us. 'We have known and believed the love that God hath to us. Herein is our love made perfect', says St John. It is the knowledge of God's love for us that enables us to love, to see and to will the good of one another. It is the knowledge that we are loved, absolutely, at the very heart of our being, which can free us from our own crippling needs and fears. That is how perfect love, God's love, casteth out fear.

We have known and believed the love that God hath to us. God's love for us, God's good will for us – that is to say God's grace – that is the starting point and the basis, and we must never lose touch with that. Let us think upon that, let us set our minds upon it and let our wills be shaped by that knowledge, for only that knowledge will enable our love.

It is significant that we celebrate marriage today, as the church has done it for many centuries, in the context of the mass. For the mass is the great allegory of love. What we represent at the altar in this service is the self-giving love of God in body broken and blood shed. 'For as often as ye eat this bread and drink this cup', says St Paul, 'you show forth the Lord's dying until he comes again.' And that body broken is to us the bread of life and that blood shed is the wine of God's new kingdom. That is the demonstration of God's love to us.

'And beloved, if God so loved us we ought also to love one another. This do and thou shalt live.'

In the name of the Father and of the Son and of the Holy Ghost.

Amen.

MARRIAGE, SECOND SERMON

This beginning of signs did Jesus in Cana of Galilee.

The first of the miracles of Jesus involved a wedding feast. Do you suppose that was accidental? I think not. It was of course a perfectly homely and ordinary occasion – just a domestic celebration in the little village of Cana – and a somewhat embarrassing one, too, when the supply of wine ran out. Jesus saved the day, apparently, by turning plain water into excellent wine. But was that all there was to it? Certainly, any embarrassed host would be grateful for such a resourceful guest; but I don't think that's entirely the point of the story.

In both the Old and New Testaments, the scriptures frequently employ the symbolism of marriage. In the prophets as well as in the Gospels, it symbolises the union between God and his people, between God and the human soul. And when Jesus comes to effect that union, the first of his signs is to manifest himself as Lord of the marriage feast, providing the good wine of spiritual joy.

When Mary, his mother, addresses him, she speaks for humanity, she speaks for thirsting souls. 'They have no wine', she says. But the good wine of God's kingdom is not simply ours to claim; it is not ours by right, and therefore he answers her: 'Woman, what have I to do with thee? Mine hour is not yet come.' In God's own time, when he wills and as he wills, his grace is given. Ours is the tasteless water of spiritual emptiness: 'They have no wine.' His is the free gift, and it is a gift which exceeds all hopes and expectations. Not as the world gives: 'Everyone at the beginning doth set forth good wine, and when men have well drunk, then that which is worse, but thou hast kept the good wine until now.'

The marriage feast is the beginning of signs – the *arche*, or principle, of signs – and it is a beginning which includes all the rest, because what it signifies is the spiritual union of humans with God, or, as St Paul says, the mystery of Christ and the Church. The true miracle, you see, is God's coming to share our humanity, that we might become partakers of his divine life. The miracle of Cana is a sign of that.

Marriage is of course a natural institution ordained by God, as old as human society, and not specifically Christian in its origins. Most of the ceremonies we associate with it derive in fact from the domestic religion of ancient Greece and Rome, and from the customs of the old Germanic tribes of Europe. And even among Christians, it was only very late, well on in the Middle Ages, that marriage came to Church, and came to be understood as a sacrament, and was provided with a liturgy. But come to Church it must, for it is indeed a sacrament – a natural sign, that is to say, of God's supernatural kingdom, signifying the bond of love which unites humans with God in Jesus Christ. And, like other sacraments, it is, for those who use it rightly, a means of the grace it signifies.

Marriage signifies a bond of love; the self-giving love of Christ for the Church. It is a matter of love: God's love for us, and our consequent love for one another. It is not fundamentally a matter of feelings, though of course they enter into it. Fundamentally, it is a matter of actively willing the eternal good of one another. That's what love means. It's not a question of effervescent feelings: it's a question of steadfast will, and therefore it takes the form of vow. It is a matter of learning and knowing what the good is, and disciplining our inclinations and intentions to that knowledge.

Thus Jeremy Taylor remarks: 'Marriage is a school and exercise of virtue; and though it hath cares, they are but instances of duty and exercises of piety. Here is the proper scene of piety and patience, of the duty of parents and the charity of relatives; here kindness is spread abroad, and love is united and made firm as a centre: marriage is the nursery of Heaven. It fills up the numbers of the elect, and hath in it the labour of love, and the delicacies of friendship, the blessing of society, and the union of hands and hearts.'

Rightly do we celebrate marriage at the altar, in the context of the mass: for the Blessed Sacrament is the sign of God's self-giving love towards us, in body broken and blood shed. As he loved us, so are we to love one another. No doubt that is a difficult vocation for all of us, whatever our state of life, and no doubt we continually fail. That is, as we say, 'only natural'. Ah, but it is the work of grace to perfect nature, to bring nature and nature's institutions, to a higher spiritual fulfilment.

We bring only the plain water of our humanity. We bring good intentions, but the fulfilment is beyond us: we have no wine. But the Lord of the marriage feast is here, and he it is who changes water into wine.

Amen.

THE ORDERING OF DEACONS

For as the rain cometh down, and the snow from heaven, and returneth not thither, but watereth the earth, and maketh it to bring forth and bud, that it may give seed to the sower and bread to the eater; So shall my word be that goeth forth out of my mouth: it shall not return to me void, but it shall accomplish that which I please, and it shall prosper in the thing whereto I sent it.

'My word which goeth forth shall not return to me void, but it shall accomplish that which I please.' Thus the prophet proclaims the mystery of the word of God: it is like the rain which cometh down from heaven, which watereth the earth, and maketh it bring forth and bud; it is like the rain from heaven, which makes fruitful the parched and barren earth. God's word goes forth into all the world, and makes that world fruitful with spiritual life, with words and deeds of truth and grace, 'seed to the sower and bread to the eater'. Thus people live most truly 'by every word that proceedeth from the mouth of God'.

But what is this word of God that goeth forth? It is the inspiration of the prophet and the vision of the seer, expressed in human words, and thus we speak of Scripture as the word of God. But the Word of God is more than words, however true and gracious they may be: words do indeed reveal the Word, but the Word is something more than words. The Word of God is nothing less than God himself. 'In the beginning was the Word, and the Word was with God, and the Word was God', says St John. The Word is God's own eternal and complete self-knowing, the perfect self-uttering of God himself. The Word is the Son of God, 'the brightness of his glory and the express image of his person'. The Word is 'God from God, Light from Light, Very God from Very God'.

The Word of God goes forth within the life of God himself – in the life of God, the Holy Trinity, God's Word, his own self-knowing, is eternally begotten. And the Word of God goes forth into the world, for 'without him was not anything made that was made'. He goes forth in all creation: 'By the Word of the Lord were the heavens made, and all the host of them by the breath of his mouth.' And in redemption, the Word of God goes forth, made flesh, to dwell amongst us, that we might behold his glory, 'the glory as of the only-begotten of the Father, full of grace and truth'. Who but St John would have dared to say it: 'we have touched and handled of the Word of Life'?

The Word of God goes forth in creation and in redemption. But the Word of God also returns. Jesus tells us in this Sunday's Gospel lesson: 'I came forth from the Father, and have come into the world: again I leave the world, and I go to the Father.' 'He that descended is the same also that ascended up, far above all heavens, that He might fill all things' – that He might complete all things, fulfill them in their spiritual destiny.

The Word of God goes forth and returns – He descends and ascends; and He does not return void or empty. He takes with him our humanity, transformed in resurrection; elevates it and returns it to that realm of spirit which is our first and final home; fills it with spiritual grace. As an ancient hymn puts it:

Yea angels tremble when they see
How changed is our humanity;
That flesh hath purged what flesh had stained,
And God, the flesh of God, hath reigned.

And Rogationtide reminds us, coming at the end of the Easter season, that the whole creation has its place in our spiritual destiny: every creature awaits with eager longing its redemption – its resurrection to serve the spiritual end for which it was created. Every creature of nature, every work of human art and science, must bring its own particular truth and beauty to the praise of God. That is its return, its spiritual destiny; and apart from that end, it remains forever frustrated, 'in bondage to corruption'. Every creature created in the going forth of the Word of God, is called to redemption in the return to that self-same Word. That uplifting of the whole creation in the ascension of our hearts and minds – that is the fundamental meaning of our prayer and worship. That is the ministry of God's Word, descending and ascending.

This evening, our bishop will ordain ministers of God's Word, and we must think about what that means. The ministry of the Word is, in the first place, not a particular vocation, not one vocation among others: it is the vocation of every one of us, and the whole of our vocation, to have our place in the going forth and the return of the Word of God. As the rain cometh down from heaven, and watereth the earth, just so the Word of God in us must fructify the earth in all the varied circumstances of human life, in every time and place; must make the earth bring forth and bud with words of truth and deeds of holy charity, to the everlasting praise of its Creator.

But in the Church, the Word of God goes forth, expressed

in a ministry of particular vocations: the Spirit's gifts are divided among us, 'severally as he will'. There must be poet and prophet and pastor and teacher, artist and craftsman, and all those walks of life which we sometimes dare to call 'ordinary'. Only by our infinite diversity can we reflect and imitate the infinite unity of God. Only thus will the Word in us fill all things, in every aspect of creation, and return it all in praise of God.

The ministry of the Word is the ministry of all of us; but within that ministry, there are particular offices and duties, among them the sacred ministries of priest and deacon, who are ordained to exercise certain functions in the Church. Those functions are manifold, of course, and not easily describable but they are first of all liturgically defined.

The office of the deacon is marked by his reading of the Gospel, and the priest's most characteristic functions are the granting of absolution and the offering of the Eucharistic sacrifice. But these liturgical acts must not be isolated: they are signs and patterns of a form of life which is necessarily in some deep sense pastoral. To read the Gospel, to proclaim the Word of God, must mean to live the Word of God in teaching and example, to build up, to edify, the body of the Lord. To pronounce God's absolution implies in every way to seek the healing of that body's wounds; to offer up the Eucharist means to gather in and offer up ourselves, our souls and bodies, to refer all life in every aspect to its spiritual end in God. Thus the Word of God goes forth into every aspect of our common life, and the Word of God returns in the transformation and uplifting of that life. The word of God goes forth, audible and visible in words and deeds and sacramental signs and does not return empty.

'It shall prosper in the thing whereto I sent it.' Thus saith the Lord, and so it is. His Word is true and faithful, and his promise does not fail. Certainly, we have disappointments and discouragements. We have our own ambitions and expectations, and often they seem sadly unrewarded.

'In the world', says Jesus, 'ye shall have tribulation.' But do not be deceived by tribulation: God's purposes do not for one moment fail or falter, however inscrutable to us their working out. Who has skill to reckon the providence of God, that perfect understanding in which 'not a sparrow falleth without your heavenly Father', that exquisite care in which every hair on your head is numbered? Who has the skill to reckon that? It is the mark of God's omnipotent goodness, says St Thomas Aquinas, that even from our evil, he makes good to come. Even our stupid mistakes, and even our sins may be, as St Paul remarks, occasions of more abundant grace. In the end, we come to bless our tribulations and trust more perfectly in the will of God. As the voice of the eagle says to the poet, in Dante's *Paradise*:

> Yet sweet to us appears our lack of skill,
> Since this good doth our good the more refine,
> That what God willeth, that we also will.

The Word of God goes forth, and does not return empty. You who come now to ordination have no doubt known, and will often know, the times in which the earth seems parched and barren, when the truth and grace of God seem far away, when doubt and dullness and your own persistent sinfulness seem to rule the day. But the Word of God goes forth, and he does not return empty, says the Prophet. As the rain from heaven, so does the Word of God descend, in raging tempest or in gentle dew, and the earth brings forth and buds. 'It shall prosper in the thing whereto I sent it.'

And therefore, I address you ordinands finally in the words of that same Prophet: 'Ye shall go out with joy, and be led forth with peace; the mountains and the hills shall break forth before you into singing, and all the trees of the field shall clap their hands.'

Amen.

THE ORDINATION OF A PRIEST

Thus saith the Lord: my word that goeth forth out of my mouth shall not return to me void, but it shall accomplish that which I please.

The rubric at the beginning of this service in the *Prayer Book* directs that 'there shall be a Sermon or Exhortation, declaring the duty and office of such as come to be admitted Priests; how necessary that Order is in the Church of Christ; and also how the people ought to esteem them in their office.'

Our English word 'priest' is derived from the Greek word '*presbuteros*', which means an 'elder' or a dignitary of some sort, as, for instance, an officer of the congregation of a synagogue, or a member of a local council. But our word 'priest' includes more than that: it includes also the meaning of the Greek word '*hiereus*', the term used by ancient pagans and Jews for the official who offers sacrifices to God, and the term used in the New Testament to refer to the sacrificial office of Christ, and the priestly character of the Christian community. Both these words are translated by our word 'priest' and both meanings are essential to our understanding of the ministry. The current fashion of reverting to the name 'presbyter' instead of 'priest' represents, therefore, a serious impoverishment of our conception of the priestly office. We must insist that our priests are not simply 'elders', or senior officers of local congregations;

they are not simply leaders or governors of parishes, they are also ministers of the sacrifice of Christ, and their office is fundamentally a liturgical one.

Certainly our priests do not offer sacrifices in the same way as did the priests of ancient Judaism or ancient paganism: we do not slay animals, nor offer other material gifts to atone for our sins and appease the wrath of God. All such ineffectual sacrifices are concluded with the cross of Christ, 'the one oblation of himself once offered', 'a full, perfect, and sufficient sacrifice, oblation and satisfaction, for the sins of the whole world.' It is that one sacrifice, and no other, which our priests represent and plead when they consecrate bread and wine at the Christian altar.

> One offering single and complete,
> With lips and heart we say;
> But what he never can repeat
> He shows forth day by day.

Our priests are ministers of the sacrifice of Christ; their duty is fundamentally the service of the altar, the showing forth of Christ's death until he come. Thus if we would understand the nature and necessity of the order of priests, we must understand the meaning of Christ's sacrifice, and our relation to it; for it is his priesthood and his sacrifice in which we share.

The priesthood of Christ is the very heart of his mission. Today, on this Feast of the Visitation of Our Lady, one of the Feasts of the Incarnation, we recall the purpose of God's coming. God's creative word is uttered in redemption; the Word of God is uttered in the world; and that Word which goeth forth does not return void or empty. He descends to humanity in order to ascend: in order to lift up, to offer up a perfected humanity to God. As the Epistle lesson for this service reminds us, 'He that descended is the same also that ascended up far above all heavens, that he might fill all things'; that he might fulfil all things, bring all things to the fulness of their spiritual destiny. That offering up humanity, that fulfilment of humanity, is the meaning of his sacrifice.

And that sacrifice, that offering up, is the basis of our spiritual life. 'When he ascended up on high … he gave gifts unto men … And he gave some, Apostles; and some, Prophets; and some, Evangelists; and some, Pastors and Teachers; for the perfecting of the saints for the work of the ministry, for the edifying of the body of Christ; till we all come, in the unity of the faith, and of the knowledge of the Son of God, unto a perfect man, unto the measure of the stature of the fulness of Christ.'

Thus Christ's sacrifice involves not just his particular, individual humanity, but the whole of human nature, the whole 'body of Christ'. It is a gathering in, and lifting up, an offering up of the whole creation, that the whole of humanity, indeed the whole of creation might find its reconciliation and fulfilment in the knowledge and love of God. That priesthood, that sacrifice, is the apostolic, prophetic, evangelistic, pastoral and teaching mission of the Church.

In this broad sense, of course, the whole Church is priestly: 'Ye are a royal priesthood, a holy nation, a peculiar people', says St Peter. We all share in the priesthood of Christ. In some sense, no doubt, we are all apostles, for we are all sent by God; we are all prophets of God's kingdom: we are all evangelists of the good news of salvation; we are all pastors to one another and teachers of one another. We all share, according to our own talents and vocations in the offering up of the world to God. We are all priests.

Yet the body of Christ is not a formless mass, without structure and distinctions. It is articulated in such a way that we share Christ's mission each in a particular sphere, in a particular way. We are 'a spiritual house', St Peter tells us; each 'living stone' has its particular place and function. And when the bishop ordains a priest, he commissions a person, and gives him grace for a very particular vocation within the priestly Church. He commissions him to pronounce with authority God's word of reconciliation, and to celebrate God's work of reconciliation liturgically at the altar.

How necessary that order is in the Church of God! As the altar is the focal point of our Church buildings, so the celebration of Christ's sacrifice must be the centre, the focal point, of our life as Christians. It is the sacramental presence of Christ, and the nutriment of that presence, which gives our life its unity and coherence. There are innumerable Christian causes, and an infinite diversity of Christian interests; what gives them coherence is that they find a common end in the offering up of Christ. Things make sense only as they are referred to their source and end in God; that is what fulfils all things; and without that, all things are ultimately aimless and fragmented in worldly incoherence. It is the office of the priest to gather us in, to reconcile us, to draw us all together spiritually in the sacrifice of Christ. Thus the priest is liturgically the symbol of Christ himself, and that is how we must esteem him in his office.

God has called Eric to be a priest; may he go joyfully to the altar of God. In a world distraught by secular incoherence and fragmentation, in a Church too often infected by the same confusions, may he be strengthened with the Spirit's gifts of wisdom and discernment, to reconcile the alien, to uphold the faltering, and gather in the wandering. Amid all the confusion of the world, may he discern the body of the Lord; 'till we all come...unto a perfect man' in the spiritual harvest of Christ's oblation.

To many in the modern world, no doubt, God's field seems choked with tares of faithlessness and perversity, so as to negate all hope of spiritual harvest. From such a standpoint, the vocation of the priest must seem nothing but folly and frustration. Worldly wisdom would hardly recommend it. But worldly wisdom does not encompass the mysteries of God. He has planted good seed, and his harvest does not fail; his word has gone forth in the world, and does not return empty. His eternal providence nourishes and surely tends us, heals us and restores us, and brings good even from our evil, in ways mysterious beyond our telling. Never for the least instant does that providence fail or falter; no least atom of creation falls outside that knowledge and that care. And, therefore, his harvest is sure.

For thus saith the Lord: 'as the rain cometh down, and the snow from heaven, and returneth not thither, but watereth the earth, and maketh it bring forth and bud, that it may give seed to the sower, and bread to the eater: so shall my word be that goeth forth out of my mouth: it shall not return to me void, but it shall accomplish that which I please, and shall prosper in the thing whereto I sent it. For ye shall go out with joy, and be led forth with peace: the mountains and the hills shall break forth before you into singing, and all the trees of the field shall clap their hands.'

Amen.

THE CONSECRATION OF A BISHOP

Jesus saith unto Peter, Simon, son of Jonas, lovest thou me? He saith unto him, Yea, Lord, thou knowest that I love thee. Jesus saith unto him, Feed my sheep.

The Gospel of St John concludes, in chapters twenty and twenty-one, with an account of the appearances of Christ, the risen Lord; and the final story there (from which our Gospel lesson comes) is about his appearance to the disciples at the Sea of Tiberias – a miraculous catch of fish, a meal together on the shore, and finally the commission to St Peter. Three times the question, 'Simon, do you love me?'; three times the challenge: 'Feed my lambs. Feed my sheep. Feed my sheep.'

That final resurrection story is a very complex one, full of rich detail and such subtleties of thought and language that no translation or exposition of it can ever seem quite adequate. The miraculous harvest of fish, for instance, is symbolic of the apostolic calling to be fishers of men: at Jesus' bidding, the barren waters are made fruitful. The breakfast on the shore is symbolic of the wedding banquet of God's Kingdom, the union of the Church with Christ, her bridegroom; the union of the redeemed soul with God; all prefigured and foretasted in the Holy Eucharist. All that symbolism – mystical and eucharistic – and much much more than that is there. But the basic point of the commission to St Peter is, after all, very simple and compelling: 'If you love me, feed my sheep.'

That is the risen Lord's commission to his Church: 'If you love me, feed my sheep.' And so, all down the centuries, by word and sacrament, the Church has fed the flock of Christ, and nourished hungry souls with a vision of that new and higher life which is God's Kingdom. It is nowadays politically correct, I know, to bewail the sins and failures of the Church, to dwell upon the evils that Christians have perpetrated, the hypocrisies of self-serving prelates, and all the cruelties and bloodshed and oppression enacted in the name of Christ.

And no doubt it is well that we should be reminded how imperfect has been, and indeed how imperfect still is our discipleship, how incomplete our wisdom is, how fragile and how limited our charity, how shameful our betrayals of our holy calling, and how necessary always must be our tears of penitence. It is well to be reminded that even at our best and truest, we have the treasure of God's kingdom in frail, earthen vessels, 'that the excellency of the power may be of God, and not of us', as St Paul puts it.

Yet the treasure is there, though it be in earthen vessels. The bread of heaven is there to nourish and sustain us, the word of God, 'sharper than any two-edged sword', penetrates our darkness and confusion with news of the risen life, and elevates our minds and hearts to heaven.

'Do not labour for the food that perishes', says Jesus, 'but for the food which endures unto life eternal', and that eternal food is none other than Christ himself, 'the bread of God ... which comes down from heaven and gives life unto the world', the very Word of God, made audible in the sacred words of revelation, made visible in holy sacraments, and manifest in holy lives. That is the substance of the apostolic commission:

to feed the flock with 'the Doctrine, Sacraments and Discipline of Christ, as the Lord hath commanded in his Holy Word'. That has always been the true mission of the Church, and that is, of course, precisely how the Church's mission was defined in our own Church's 'Solemn Declaration' a century ago. May we be steadfast in that commitment.

Surely the divine commission re-echoes in our minds as we gather here tonight for the consecration of a bishop in the Church of God. No doubt, the functions of a bishop are manifold; but, above all, he is to be the shepherd of Christ's flock in this place, the overseer or stewards of God's household here; and to him especially is directed the challenge, 'If you love me, feed my sheep.' And that must be an intimidating challenge in these days of a troubled Church in a troubled world. The bishop must somehow be a focus of unity in a Church threatened by the Scylla and Charybdis of radical schism on the one hand, and a vacuous bureaucratic uniformity on the other. He will be under constant pressure to conform to the faddish standards and inclinations of the present age in the Church and in the world; he will be tempted often towards discouragement, and even cynicism; and there won't be many easy answers. In fact, there will be only one real answer, and that one won't always be easy. St Paul says it, in First Corinthians: 'It is required in stewards that one be found faithful.' And as St Irenaeus, the great exponent of apostolic succession in the midst of the Gnostic crisis of the second century, clearly saw and said, the bishop can serve as a focus of unity only inasmuch as he himself is faithful to the tradition of the truth divinely given; only thus can he hold the freedom and integrity of mind which can resist the pressures to conform to the spirit of the present age.

These are difficult and trying times for the Church, no

doubt; 'a day of clouds and thick darkness'; and yet, it is easy to exaggerate that aspect of things. Certainly, the Church has often seen much darker days, and has come through her trials purified and renewed, refined as though by fire. Examples of faithfulness through tribulation are abundant in Holy Scripture and through the centuries of the Church's history. I've been thinking a good deal recently about an episcopal example, which it seems to me appropriate to recall on this occasion: that of St Gregory, the late-sixth-century Bishop of Rome, who, in the year 596, sent St Augustine and forty monks to England to found the See of Canterbury.

As one of his biographers put it:

> Gregory did his great work and lived his noble life in the midst of circumstances which might well have daunted even the most heroic … On one side the swords of the barbarians hemmed him in, on the other he was exposed to the unscrupulous animosity of Imperial officials. Few sympathised with him, hardly any understood him. Amid starving people, mutinous soldiers, greedy officials, intriguing bishops, untrustworthy agents, in the ruined capital of a desolated country he stood alone, without support save in his conscience and his God.

And yet, in that age of almost unimaginable ruin, his work was immensely creative in educing from chaos the shape of European Christendom, intellectual, moral and institutional.

'In the midst of the unsteady flow of time', said Gregory, 'the man of God knows how to keep steady the steps of his mind.' But just how is that possible? I think the Venerable Bede penetrated the secret of it, when he reported how Gregory, 'amid the incessant battering of worldly cares', strove to be 'fastened, as by the cable of an anchor, to the peaceful shore of prayer'.

The tasks of the Church, and therefore of the bishop, are indeed challenging, beyond all human competence, but in the doctrine, sacraments and discipline of Christ our Saviour, faithfully delivered into our hands by those who were in Christ before us, and with our souls firmly anchored on 'the peaceful shore of prayer', we have all we need, and more. 'Not that we are sufficient of ourselves to think anything as of ourselves', as St Paul says, 'but our sufficiency is of God, who hath also made us able ministers of the new covenant.' 'Be of good cheer', says Jesus, 'I have overcome the world.'

May sound faith, good courage, and unshakable confidence in the blessed providence of God be with you all; with Tony and Anna, and with all you faithful people here, as you enter upon a new stage in your pilgrimage. 'Follow after righteousness, godliness, faith, love, patience, meekness. Fight the good fight of faith. Lay hold upon eternal life.'

And now, to God the Holy Trinity, the blessed and only Sovereign, the King of Kings and Lord of Lords, Good Shepherd of his flock, be honour and glory everlasting.

Amen.

THE INDUCTION OF A RECTOR

One thing is needful.

The purpose of our gathering here tonight, as the bishop has reminded us in his exhortation, is that your new rector might be given institution into the cure of souls in this parish. And since the charge of immortal souls is so solemn and weighty a thing, we have been bidden to pray for God's grace that he may perform aright the duties which pertain to so sacred and grave a trust.

The charge of immortal souls: it is indeed a solemn and weighty thing; it is indeed a grave and sacred trust. And surely, one might add, it is a fearsomely difficult thing, especially in an age which knows little about immortal souls, and cares little for their cure.

The charge of immortal souls: I wonder if we can even understand anymore what those solemn words mean. What on earth are we up to? I think it must be the obligation of the preacher on such an occasion as this to try to make some sense of this charge – to try to say something about what it can and must mean for both priest and people.

And that is a task both simple and difficult – in the same way in which the Gospel itself is at once both supremely simple and immeasurably difficult: simple, because only one thing is needful; difficult, because to understand that one thing is really to understand everything; and to purchase that one treasure is to sell all that you have.

One thing is needful. As you will, no doubt, have recognized, that text comes from the Gospel story of Mary and Martha. Jesus had come to Bethany to visit his good friends of the household of Lazarus: and Martha busied herself with the demand of hospitality, while her sister Mary sat down at Jesus' feet to hear his word.

Martha, 'cumbered with much serving' asked Jesus to tell Mary to help her, and Jesus responded with the rather strange answer from which our text comes:

> Martha, Martha, you are careful and troubled about many things; but one thing is needful; and Mary has chosen that better part which shall not be taken away from her.

A strange answer, surely. Martha serves, while Mary takes a holiday – and Mary he says, has chosen 'the better part'. One's immediate sympathy is surely with Martha. What after all can be above the faithful fulfilment of the demands of duty and charity? What 'better part' has Mary chosen? What one thing is needful?

In the ancient tradition of biblical interpretation, Martha and Mary were seen as the types or patterns of active and contemplative life. This distinction between active and contemplative life was of course, by no means new with the Christian Gospel, nor peculiar to it. The tradition of Greek philosophy held the distinction, and also the judgement, that contemplation was the better part. 'Final felicity is the pure contemplation of the noblest truth', said Aristotle, in his *Ethics*. And many a Father of the early Church spoke of himself, in terms familiar to the Greeks, as seeking the *theoretikos bios,* the philosophic life of contemplation. Very deep in the fibre of Christian civilization – though no doubt somewhat alien from us today – is the conviction that the highest form of human and Christian activity is the contemplative life.

But what is it about, this contemplative life, and what sense does it make? And what has it to do with the life of a parish in the twentieth century? These contemplatives, these 'souls on holiday', as a medieval poet so poignantly calls them, may be all very well; but in the world we know, perhaps souls at work with the intensity of practical charity would seem to be more needful; and how can we keep our eyes fixed upon the heavenly Jerusalem which is free, when all our earthly Jerusalems are in bondage with their children – when we are they upon whom the end of the world is come? Yet, says St Paul, that most eminently practical of men, 'our conversation is in Heaven'.

'One thing is needful, and Mary has chosen the better part.'

So goes the contradiction, and I think that for modern Christians, it is a very painful contradiction, in so far as they remain at all attached to the traditions of Christian spirituality and 'other worldliness'. Contemplation looks like a kind of 'copping out'; worship seems a kind of luxury for those who happen to enjoy it, or feel that they get something out of it.

But I think that is to misunderstand the nature of contemplation, to misunderstand what worship is all about. Contemplation is not a leaving behind of the world as much as it is a gathering together and holding together of the world in the vision, the knowledge of its divine source and end. It is the activity of returning the world to God in knowledge and love. The many things about which Martha is careful and troubled fall apart into incoherence; in Mary's contemplation of the divine word, they cohere in the vision of God's providence. This is what is so superbly put in the final Canto of Dante's vision of Heaven, the *Paradiso*, where he says:

> In that abyss I saw how love held bound
> Into one volume all the leaves whose flight
> Is scattered through the universe around;
> ...
> For everything the will has ever sought
> Is gathered there, and there is every quest
> Made perfect, which apart from it falls short.

There is a peculiar superstition about to the effect that it is important to be doing as many things as possible – that we should be in continual gyration, frantically dancing to the rhythm of every drummer – that happiness and freedom are to be found in the infinity of experience, in the multiplicity of things with which Martha is 'cumbered'.

But we must not squander our substance in that way: we need not buy every plastic pearl on the market, there is one pearl of great price. We must not follow every spirit, but we must test the spirits, whether they be of God. For even if we were to gain the whole world, what would it profit us? The world is not enough for immortal souls. Truth and freedom are to be found in the world of experience only when that experience can be seen in the light of contemplation's vision of the providence of God. 'Mary has chosen the better part.'

The Church is 'cumbered with much serving'. It is careful and troubled about many things; it wants to make people good; it wants to develop the world and make it a better place. Sometimes it is so anxious to be relevant to this world that it seems ready to jump on any passing bandwagon, to accommodate itself to every fancy and fad of this present age. Even our worship can become distorted, so that we come to think of it as a technique to be used for some sort of psychological manipulation of ourselves or of other people. And even when we begin to wake up to the fact, as so many people seem now to be doing, that our real problems are those of spirituality, even then we imagine that it is a matter of rummaging about the world for new and different techniques, whether they be psychological or chemical, while day by day, from one Sunday morning until the next, most of our Churches stand empty, and the voice of praise is silent. Nay rather let the Church praise God seven whole days.

Surely the Church knows better than that. Alas, the fabulous wings unused! And how strange it is that we trust the powers that ruin, and not the powers that bless.

But never despair of the Church. We are, after all, the people of God, born anew, and endowed with the rich gifts of the spirit. Despite our wanderings, the Church has a wisdom which is sure, against which the gates of hell can never prevail. And the Church has, after all, a sublime practicality which knows how to transform the bread and wine of our spiritual poverty into the glorious banquet of the Lord.

Your rector has been charged with the cure of immortal souls and you are asked to support him in this solemn and weighty thing. How will you do this? Will this be a place where day by day the voice of praise is heard, where it is manifest that the worship of God is first? Not because it will make us better, not because it will develop the world but only because God is God, and he is to be known and loved, worshipped and adored. That is the one thing needful.

I pray that you may have grace to choose that better part, which shall not be taken from you.

Amen.

A THANKSGIVING FOR RESTORATION OF A CHURCH BUILDING

O how amiable are thy dwellings, thou Lord of hosts! My soul hath a desire and longing to enter into the courts of the Lord: my heart and my flesh rejoice in the living God.

Tonight, we recall the disaster which struck St George's Church three years ago and we celebrate with thanksgiving the wonderful work of renewal and restoration which has gone on here since then. We celebrate this lovely house of God, this 'amiable dwelling', in which, once again, we are privileged to worship. We celebrate the joys of the temple:

> Hallowed this dwelling where the Lord abideth
> This is none other than the gate of heaven
> Strangers and pilgrims, seeking homes eternal
> Pass through its portals.

So sang an anonymous ninth-century poet, celebrating the sacred mystery of the Church.

But what, really, do we mean by such a celebration? Surely we know that God, eternal and infinite, does not dwell in a temple made with hands. 'Behold, the heaven, and the heaven of heavens cannot contain thee; how much less the house that

I have builded', said King Hezekiah, speaking of the temple of Jerusalem. And remember what Jesus told the Samaritan woman, when she asked about the proper place of worship: 'God is Spirit', he said, 'and those who worship him must worship him in spirit and in truth'.

And yet, in the holy scriptures, the temple is never really a matter of indifference. Of course, God does not dwell in temples made with hands; and yet, the earthly temple stands as sign and symbol of the coming of the Lord, and his presence in our midst. God is Spirit, and he is not confined by finite, earthly forms; and yet, God is incarnate, God is enfleshed in Jesus Christ, he tabernacles with us, in body and blood, in bread and wine; the finite particulars of time and place become reflection, and manifestation, and vehicles of his eternal glory. 'We have seen his glory', says St John, 'the glory as of the only-begotten of the Father, full of grace and truth'. 'We have touched and handled of the world of life.' 'Behold the tabernacle of God is with men.'

God is Spirit, but the Spirit makes himself visible, and audible, and tangible in earthly forms. The Spirit breathes over the barren waters of chaos and vacuity, and gives form and definition; he shapes us into a visible temple of the Lord, a temple of living stones, a spiritual house of God. Of that spiritual house, the church building is sign and symbol. The ancient Latin gradual verse for the mass of Dedication, which we've heard this evening in Anton Bruckner's lovely setting, speaks of the Church as '*inestimabile sacramentum*': 'inestimable sacrament'; 'outward and visible sign of inward and spiritual grace'.

Thus the earthly temple, the visible house of God, is not just a convenient meeting-place for the practice of religion; it means so much more than that. It is sign and sacrament of the spiritual community: the 'spiritual house' of which St Peter speaks, 'a royal priesthood, a holy nation, a people for God's own possession'.

And not only that: it is also sign of the house of God within us, for we ourselves, as St Peter puts it, are 'living temples' of the Lord, called to be 'holy and acceptable to him'. Our very souls are to be sanctuaries of his presence. The building is a sign of all that and more: it is sign and symbol of a higher life, the meeting of the soul with God in knowledge and in love; it is sign and symbol of a higher citizenship, the life of heaven. That is why the ancient temple in Jerusalem was gloriously adorned, and that is why Christian churches all down the centuries, have been adorned with all the best we have to offer. 'The hill of Zion is a fair place, and the joy of the whole earth.'

Thus the twelfth-century abbot, Suger, at the dedication of the great new abbey church of St Denis, in Paris – the very first Gothic building – caused to be inscribed upon the doors these lines: 'Bright is the noble work, and being nobly bright, the work should brighten minds, so that they may travel through these earthly lights to the true light where Christ is the true door.' '*Inestimabile sacramentum*': the church is sign and symbol, to inspire us, and lead us on, to draw our sluggish, earth-bound minds to higher things, to that temple not made with hands, the heavenly 'Jerusalem, which is above and free, and the mother of us all'. It is symbol of the Spirit's homeland. 'My soul hath a desire and longing to enter into the courts of the Lord: my heart and my flesh rejoice in the living God.'

We celebrate with thankfulness this evening a great work of renewal and restoration underway here in this place. And as we do so, let us be reminded that this visible renewal has its true significance as a sacrament; as an outward sign of a renewal of the Spirit. What is truly important here is that the Word of God is faithfully proclaimed, and that God is worshipped in holiness and beauty, and served in the persons of our neighbours. Such matters are the very heart of spiritual renewal for community and individual. The life of common prayer, the life of penitential adoration: those are the springs from which will flow the virtues of faith and hope and charity; those are the springs whose waters wash away the dreary dust of worldliness, and renew the face of the earth. 'All my fresh springs are in thee', cries the Psalmist.

Renewal means a deepening of our life of prayer: 'My house shall be called the house of prayer', says Jesus. Renewal means lifting our eyes to look upon our Spirit's home, the new and free Jerusalem, which is above, of which this building is a sacrament; and we must know that we are strangers here and pilgrims. That is the renewal of the temple, the rebuilding of God's house, among us and within us; and that must be the inner meaning of our celebration.

'One thing have I desired of the Lord, which I will require: even that I may dwell in the house of the Lord all the days of my life, to behold the fair beauty of the Lord and to visit his temple.'

Amen.

Giovanni Pisano, *Cardinal Virtues supported by Faith, Hope, and Charity,* 12th-13th century, Holy Water Font, Fuorcivitas.

THE UNIVERSITY AND THE SPIRIT

I say then, walk in the Spirit.

It is, of course, purely accidental that the university service occurs this year within the week of the thirteenth Sunday after Trinity, and that our Epistle and Gospel lessons are therefore those appointed for that week: in the epistle lesson we have St Paul's exhortation to Christians in ancient Galatia, that they should 'walk in the Spirit'; and the gospel lesson is about love of God and neighbour, concluding with Jesus' story about the Good Samaritan. We could perhaps sum up the message of those lessons in one simple sentence: life in the Spirit – spiritual life – is life lived in the perspective of love of God and neighbour; it is the life of charity.

But what has that to do with the university? Is there any more specific message there for us, as we enter upon a new academic year? St Paul begins by warning us against what he calls 'the works of the flesh': 'adultery, fornication, uncleanness, lasciviousness, idolatry, witchcraft, hatred, variance, emulations, wrath, strife, seditions, heresies, envyings, murders, drunkenness, revellings and such like'. Quite a list, and most of the items not totally unfamiliar in our experience of college life. But what, really, are these 'works of the flesh'?

Some of you may recall those chapters in Book XIV of *The City of God*, where St Augustine, in an argument against Vergil and the Platonists, discusses this text, and explains that the 'works of the flesh' must always be seen as essentially perversions of will: willing self-indulgence, willing exploitations of others, willing worldliness. And such perversions of will are certainly familiar enough to all of us. We share in a world deeply scarred by sins of self-indulgence, greed and exploitation; we are the children of a century which has perpetrated cruelty and violence to a degree unimagined in the darkest ages of our past. And St Paul is saying that the remedy does not lie in some legal system, but in a conversion of will – a new spiritual life – the life of charity.

It is precisely about that conversion of will that Jesus speaks in our gospel lesson, when the lawyer asks him what he must do to inherit eternal life. Jesus tells him that he must love God with all his heart and soul and mind and strength, and love his neighbour as he loves his own self. 'This do, and thou shalt live.' This 'love' of which Jesus speaks is not a matter of emotional attachment, or the bonds of natural affection – his story of the Good Samaritan makes that point clearly: it is crucial to the story that the hero is not a Jew, but a Samaritan, a stranger and outcast, for whom those attachments do not exist. The love of which Jesus speaks is charity: the steadfast willing of the good – the absolute and eternal good which is God and in that perspective, willing the good of one another.

That, I think, is the basic meaning of our scripture readings, and it seems to me a meaning profoundly relevant to our human condition, at all times and in all places. But we must also try to see its particular relevance to the life of the university and to our vocation as scholars.

The university exists for the cultivation of what our philosophical tradition since Aristotle has called the 'intellectual virtues' – the various forms of science and wisdom; it is an institution dedicated to the pursuit of truth. But the truth and the Good are finally inescapable: the truth is simply the good of intellect, and all the virtues are summed up in that steadfast willing of the good which we call charity. Thus charity is said to be the 'form' of all the virtues: the form in which all of them have actual life. And it involves a dialectical interplay, a reciprocity, an interdependence of intellect and will. To love the truth, you must know it, but to know the truth you must love it. That is the doctrine which you will find adumbrated in the *Ethics* of Aristotle, and more fully worked out in the trinitarian doctrine of St Augustine, in the scholastic theology of the thirteenth century, and in the poetry of Dante.

Loving depends upon knowing, and knowing depends upon loving. That dialectical formula stands at the very heart of the great tradition of Christian humanism in which our universities were founded. The unity and creative interplay of diverse elements and aspects and dimensions – intellectual, moral, religious – belonged to the very essence of that tradition, and it is of course precisely that unity that has tended to be lost in the modern secularizing of so many universities. And that loss seems to me a very sad impoverishment and narrowing of vision. St Paul was surely right when he said that without charity, knowledge was worthless: 'sounding brass and tinkling cymbal'.

The same point is made, I think quite dramatically by a remarkable piece of thirteenth-century sculpture, and I'll describe it for you as a concluding illustration. It's a work by Giovanni Pisano, the very greatest of Gothic sculptors, contemporary of St Thomas Aquinas, and Dante and Giotto, noted, for instance, for his work on the façade of Siena Cathedral, where he placed figures of Plato and Aristotle, engaged in lively conversation with ancient Hebrew kings and prophets and ancient sibyls – illustrating magnificently the interplay of human philosophy and divine revelation and human religious aspiration. It's a wonderful illustration of Christian humanism.

But the particular work I want to focus upon is less well-known. It's a font the youthful Giovanni Pisano created for the church of San Giovanni Fuorcivitas, in the Tuscan city of Pistoia. Around the bowl of the font, he carved figures representing the four natural (or cardinal) virtues: prudence, justice, temperance and fortitude; and for the pedestal, he carved faith, hope and charity. It's a very humanistic statement, in that the new life at baptism is seen as a renewal of the natural human virtues; but at the same time, it's a powerful affirmation that the restoration of authentic humanity depends upon and is sustained by, the supernatural virtues of faith, hope, and charity. Thus it seems to me a marvellous illustration of what today's scripture lessons are about, and what we might well have in mind as we enter upon a new academic year: the authentic life of intellect is grounded in and sustained by charity.

And of course it is profoundly right that we mark the beginning with this liturgy, in which we are invited to eat and drink the charity of God.

'I say, then, walk in the Spirit.'

Amen.

A UNIVERSITY MATRICULATION SERVICE

Wisdom hath builded her house, she hath hewn out her seven pillars ... she hath also furnished her table.

The task of the preacher at this matriculation service has several dimensions. In the first place, the sermon must be, as always, an attempt to draw out the meaning of the scripture lessons appointed for today in the Church's calendar; but it must also have some special reference and relevance to the academic occasion which brings many of us here this evening. To some, perhaps, the ceremony of matriculation seems somewhat mysterious; matriculation, after all, is nothing else than registration, and surely we finished that business long ago. Our word 'matriculation' derives from the Latin term '*matricula*', which means a public register or an official list – not, I think, from '*matriculus*', which means 'an unknown fish'. What we are observing this evening is just the ceremonial side of registration, adding a certain dimension of solemnity to what might otherwise seem a purely routine and bureaucratic exercise. And thus, the ceremony of matriculation extends to all of us an invitation to think seriously about the significance of our entering into the life of the university.

It is of course purely a matter of coincidence that this year matriculation occurs in the twentieth Sunday after Trinity, so that we have the particular scripture lessons we've just heard, from the epistle to the Ephesians and St Matthew's Gospel. It's pure coincidence; but how appropriate they seem, with their emphasis upon grasping opportunity, upon pursuing wisdom with seriousness, sobriety and humility, 'redeeming the time.' In the gospel lesson, Jesus says that the kingdom of heaven – God's kingdom of spiritual life – is like a wedding banquet, to which many were invited. Some made light of the invitation, and some even slew the messengers, and were themselves destroyed. But the wedding was furnished with guests, including one who did not wear a wedding garment; that is to say, one who did not put on the special robe the host provided; one who did not accept his host's generosity, nor his own status as a guest, and was therefore cast out into outer darkness, with weeping and gnashing of teeth.

The story is of course a parable; it's really a story, as Jesus says, about the kingdom of heaven – a story about the mystic banquet of the Son of God, the feast of spiritual truth and spiritual life to which we are invited, and to which we can come only with seriousness of purpose and humility of heart. And that prescription is simply underlined in the epistle lesson with its talk of sobriety, thanksgiving and mutual subjection.

Now all of this is quite directly relevant to the life of the university, and to understanding our purpose here; for surely the real point of our institution is to set out wisdom's banquet, the nutriment of the life of the human spirit. 'Wisdom hath builded her house, she hath hewn out her seven pillars … she hath also furnished her table.' We are called here to wisdom's banquet, the *convivium* of *sapientia*.

In the twelfth-century – that great age of intellectual and

artistic renaissance, in which our university traditions have their roots, a certain Honorius Augustodunensis wrote a little treatise precisely on this subject. He called it, *De anima exsilio et patria:* 'On the Exile and Homeland of the Soul.' The exile of the soul, he says, the Egyptian bondage of the soul, is ignorance. The road to freedom is a journey, which he traces in detail, through the cities of the seven liberal arts – the seven pillars of wisdom's house, wherein Priscian and Donatus teach grammar; Cicero teaches rhetoric; Aristotle, dialectic; Boethius, arithmetic and music; and so on, until we arrive at length at the *superna civitas*, the heavenly Jerusalem, the free city of the Spirit, where wisdom – *sapientia* – has prepared a *convivium* – a banquet.

The idea of education as liberation and nutriment of Spirit has been basic to the whole conception of the university in our traditions. Spiritual freedom, spiritual nutriment, founded in faith and understanding – founded in faith understood – has been the whole point and purpose of the Christian university.

When that point is lost, or obscured, as it tends to be in the modern secularizing of our institutions, the university all too readily comes to be seen as serving only immediate worldly aims and social utility. All too readily, it becomes merely a reflection of contemporary opinions and conventions, the slave of fads and fancies, and all the shibboleths of political correctness. I hope that our university is something better than that, and that it will be something better than that for those of you who are matriculated here today. I hope it will help you to attain a measure of spiritual freedom and discernment, some higher and broader perspectives, some renewal of the mind, which will free you at least a little bit from the conventional assumptions and the narrow conformities of the present age.

That is what this chapel stands for – spiritual freedom and

spiritual nutriment – for here, in word and sacrament, in sign and symbol, is day by day proclaimed and set before us the message of a world overcome, the pledge and foretaste of the wedding banquet of the Lamb, true Wisdom's *convivium*. Here there is brought into focus the true vocation of the university, the cultivation of the life of the Spirit. If you catch even a glimpse of that calling as your own, your time here will have been worthwhile.

Wisdom hath builded her house, she hath hewn out her seven pillars … she hath also furnished her table. Therefore, see then that ye walk circumspectly, not as fools, but as wise, redeeming the time, because the days are evil.

Amen.

THE UNIVERSITY AND THE TRANSFIGURATION

We have also a more sure word of prophecy; whereunto ye do well that ye take heed, as unto a light that shineth in a dark place, until the day dawn, and the day star arise in your hearts.

A college reunion is appropriately, and perhaps inevitably, an occasion for nostalgia. But I think that it is not only nostalgia that binds us all together here at King's, as members of this community of memory and hope which is our university. I think we are united by our experience of a certain kind of education, and also, I hope, by certain common convictions about educational ideals.

There are some, no doubt, for whom learning suggests a simple transfer of information from book to mind, or from mind to mind. For others – as, indeed, for the ancient sophists, but also for vast numbers of our contemporaries – it suggests the cultivation of cleverness, and the acquisition of technical or professional skills of one sort or another. But the existence of such a university as ours presupposes a much broader view of education; for such an institution is obviously concerned with the moral and intellectual formation of the whole human being, an enterprise in which not only the classroom, but also this chapel, and all the myriad activities of the shared life of the community have a part. The whole life of the whole community is the real curriculum.

It's not just a matter of information gained, or skills acquired: if that is all there is, the potential for destructiveness is as great as that for creativity. A deeper dimension of education – a deeper dimension of understanding and motivation – is required.

Edward Pusey of Oxford, nearly a century and a half ago, put the matter this way:

> The object of a university is not simply or mainly to cultivate the intellect. Intellect, by itself, heightened, sharpened, refined, cool, piercing, subtle, would be after the likeness, not of God, but of His enemy, who is acuter and subtler far, than the acutest and subtlest. The object of universities is, with and through the discipline of the intellect, as far as may be, to discipline and train the whole moral and intelligent being. The problem and special work of a university is, not how to advance science, not how to make discoveries, not to form new schools of mental philosophy, nor to invent new modes of analysis, not to produce works in Medicine, Jurisprudence, or even Theology; but to form minds religiously, morally, intellectually, which shall discharge aright whatever duties God, in His Providence, shall appoint them.

Perhaps it sounds old-fashioned to say so – indeed, I think it sounded old-fashioned at Oxford a century and a half ago – but it is nevertheless true that our fundamental need is to be educated in virtue; educated in the Good. As St Paul reminds us, without knowledge and love of the everlasting good, without charity, all our information and all our skills are really 'nothing worth' – just 'sounding brass and tinkling cymbals', just noisy and destructive nonsense, which 'profiteth nothing'.

Knowledge and love of the everlasting Good: for Christian understanding, that Good is not just a perfect and transcendent principle, an ideal beyond all human comprehension. For Christians, the supreme and perfect and eternal Good is made incarnate, embodied and manifest in Jesus Christ. The Good is audible and visible and tangible in word and sacrament. As St John puts it so strikingly, 'we have touched and handled of the Word of Life'. This chapel exists in the midst of the university to hold before our minds and hearts the vision of the pure and perfect good made flesh, that we might form our lives accordingly – that we might touch and handle of the Word of Life.

In this regard, the scripture lessons for today seem singularly appropriate for this occasion. Peter and James and John witnessed the Lord transfigured, upon the holy mount, 'and behold, there appeared unto them Moses and Elijah talking with Him'. Peter wanted to build three tabernacles: one for Jesus, one for Moses, and one for Elijah. But 'a bright cloud overshadowed them: and behold a voice out of the cloud which said, "This is my beloved Son, in whom I am well pleased; Hear ye Him".' And then, 'when they had lifted up their eyes, they saw no one, save Jesus only.'

Moses and the law of God, Elijah and all the holy prophets of Israel, are united and fulfilled in the Son of God, the Word of God made flesh – united and fulfilled in the vision of a new and risen life. 'Tell the vision to no one', says Jesus, 'until the Son of Man be risen again from the dead'. It is his resurrection, you see, which substantiates the vision. It is that vision of transfiguration which must constitute the wellspring of truly Christian education, and of Christian spiritual life in Church and society.

Our university is not a secular institution, existing to embody the spirit of the present age or the transitory convenience of contemporary society. Those brave souls who founded it, two centuries ago, were voluntary exiles from their homeland, for the sake of principles which they esteemed more highly than any convenience or prosperity. Even in those desperate days, one of their most urgent concerns was for truly Christian education, that there might be a succession of good and wise leaders for Church and state. We are their successors, and that is our tradition.

But tradition is not a static thing. It is a living and a growing thing, and certainly the tradition of this college has often shown, and still does show, its flexibility.

As the Reverend W. B. King, then Rector of St Luke's Church, Halifax, remarked during the centennial celebrations a century ago, 'The College must possess to a very great extent the secret of recuperation, else she could never have reached her present standing.' A good tradition has a growing edge, and assimilates changes while the fundamental principles remain the same. As St Paul advises the Thessalonians, 'Quench not the spirit. Despise not prophesyings.' Don't retreat before the challenges of the new and unexpected. But also, don't be carried away by every novel wind: 'Prove all things', test all things, criticise and weigh all things – 'Hold fast to what is good.' That activity of proving is very much the duty of the university.

Certainly, our knowledge is always partial: 'we know in part', says St Paul, 'and we prophesy in part'. 'We see through a glass darkly', as one might see an image in a clouded mirror. We who hold the vision of life transfigured; we, with all creation, await with eager longing the revealing of the sons of God. Then we shall see face to face, and know as we are known. In the meantime, as St Peter puts it in today's Epistle lesson we have the sure word of prophecy in the vision of transfiguration: 'whereunto ye do well that ye take heed, as unto a light that shineth in a dark place, until the day dawn, and the day star arise in your hearts.'

Amen.

A UNIVERSITY BACCALAUREATE SERVICE

We know in part, and we prophesy in part.

'All men by nature desire to know.' So Aristotle begins his great work of theology, which we call the *Metaphysics*. 'All men by nature desire to know', he says – above all to know the causes, the reasons, the principles which inform our whole experience, and which constitute our very being. According to 'The Philosopher', this desire to know, this seeking for the fundamental reasons, underlies and motivates the cultivation of all our arts and sciences, which, in their several ways, are all tributaries of that highest wisdom which knows and wills all things in the perfect unity of their source and end, and sees all things *sub specie aeternitatis*. 'All men desire to know', and in the attainment of that highest wisdom consists our highest and most perfect happiness, he says, for it is the fulfilment, the actuality of what is most divine in us.

Thus, in wisdom, we may share, somehow, the very life of God; we strive to scale Olympus, where, as Homer says, the gods forever dwell in perfect peace, where the serene air is never riled by any earthly storm, where every riddle is resolved, and every conflict reconciled. It is a winsome and a noble vision, this paradise of contemplation. But this vision of a pure and perfect science, this vision of the free and perfect life of intellect, is also, as Aristotle knows, essentially a tragic vision; for the life of gods, he says, is, after all, a life too high for humans. We cannot be as gods, it seems – that is diabolical presumption; we ascend in contemplation and gaze upon the meadows of Elysium, but we must drink of Lethe, and forget, and descend once more into the dividedness and incoherence of all our partial knowings. 'For we know in part.'

'All men by nature desire to know' – to know the reasons and the principles of things; and that is the meaning of our universities. They are offspring of the 'School of Athens', translated into other times and places. In and through all the particular occupations of our arts and sciences, we seek a universe of thought, a paradise of wisdom, coherent and complete – we seek somehow to be as gods.

But in the world of Christendom, our universities are not just Schools of Athens in translation. In their origin and their essential character, they are something else as well; they depend – quite radically depend – upon another doctrine. St Thomas, in the first question of his *Summa* of theology, asks whether, besides those philosophical disciplines which human reason can investigate, some other doctrine is required. And he answers that because our final happiness depends upon a knowledge which exceeds our finite reason's comprehension, our salvation must depend upon God's own revelation, which we appropriate by faith.

'We know in part and we prophesy in part.' And the School of Prophecy must redeem the School of Athens. By faith we grasp the charity of God revealed, the substance of our hope, the evidence of what our reason does not see, except in part. By faith we grasp the charity of God, which opens up to us a paradise of wisdom – not as a momentary vision, of which a draught of Lethe must deprive us, but as our veritable home as sons of God and heirs of life eternal. Thus the School of Athens, the community of thought, is born again, and its proxies are the theological virtues of faith and hope and charity.

It is in the revelation of infinite, eternal Good in Christ our Lord – the charity of God made visible to faith – that we find coherence and renewal of the mind, the principle, the starting-point of new understanding. That greatest of Christian poets, who understood better than most the essential tragedy of pagan speculation, speaks of this new vision as he approaches the glory of the blessed Trinity, in the *Paradiso*:

> In that abyss I saw how love held bound
> Into one volume all the leaves whose flight
> Is scattered through the universe around;
>
> . . .
>
> For everything the will has ever sought
> Is gathered there, and there is every quest
> Made perfect, which apart from it falls short.

We know in part, of course; and we prophesy in part; we see, says Saint Paul, through a glass darkly – as one might see an image in a clouded mirror; but as he puts it in today's epistle lesson, we who have the first fruits of the Spirit, along with all creation, await with eager longing the revelation of the sons of God. Then we shall see face to face, and know as we are known. Our desire to know will be resolved in the charity of God.

Thus in the old tradition of our universities, the theology of revelation is the very heart, *regina artium*, and queen of sciences; for it is theology's prophetic vision which redeems our quest, and enables us by faith and understanding, to see one end of all our occupations, and thus to be a 'uni-versity'. That tradition has been drastically eroded, to be sure, and the consequences are drastic too, I think, both for the university and for theology. The university too readily becomes a mere diversity of training schools, one of which might even be theology. We lose prophetic vision, and too readily mistake a vacillating conformity to the present age for renewal of the mind. All in the name of practicality, of course! But what is genuinely practical, except what redeems our knowing and our aspiration from confusion and despair, from empty secularity which bores itself to death?

To those of you who will be graduated here today, and who have departed so far from College custom as to elect this year a home-grown preacher, so to speak, I must attempt to say some special word as valedictory. 'Encaenia', as no doubt you know, means a beginning, a commencement. And as you now begin in varied circumstances, some new phase of life and education – in the 'real' world, some would say – your preacher ought to offer fatherly advice. But let me say just this: I hope that in our common life at King's, we have managed to preserve and to communicate, however haltingly, enough of the true tradition of the university – the School of Athens and the School of Prophecy – that you will never be the slaves of shallow practicality, conformists to the present age, but will ever seek renewal of the mind, will ever seek to understand that everlasting reason which all men by nature must desire and which the charity of God reveals.

Our final meeting here, on your graduation day, is most fittingly the Christian liturgy. We celebrate the charity of God in the sacrifice of Christ our Lord, that we may touch and handle of the Word of Life, that we might be partakers of divinity. We make that charity our food and drink, that he may dwell in us and we in him. We know in part, and we prophesy in part. Now we know in part and prophesy in part; but one day we shall know as we are known.

Amen.

A SERMON ON PRAYER

Seeing, then, that we have a great high priest, that is passed into the heavens, Jesus, the Son of God, let us hold fast our profession. Let us come boldly unto the throne of grace, that we may obtain mercy, and find grace to help in time of need.

All human desire, all human longing and aspiration, expressed in a thousand different forms and at a thousand different levels, is ultimately the desire for God, and prayer is simply the articulation of that desire. Indeed, the desire is itself the substance of prayer, as St Augustine remarks in one of his sermons, 'Desire itself prays, even if the tongue be still. If always you desire, always you pray.'

'When does prayer sleep? Only when desire grows cold.' St Thomas makes the same point, in his commentary on First Thessalonians, when he says that the desire itself has the force of prayer, and Richard Hooker, in the *Laws of Ecclesiastical Polity*, remarks that 'Every good and holy desire, though it lack the form, hath notwithstanding in itself the substance, and with him the force of prayer, who regardeth the very moanings, groans, and sighs of the heart of man.'

Our prayer is our desire, whether articulate or dumb. But to such an account of prayer as human aspiration, Christian theology would add another and more profound dimension, in the recognition of prayer as divine gift. St Augustine makes the point in a famous passage at the beginning of the *Confessions*, where he says, 'It is thou, O God, who dost rouse mankind to delight in praising thee, for thou hast made us for thyself, and our hearts are restless until they find their rest in thee.' Later on, in Book XIII, he comments more fully upon the meaning of the restless heart. 'My love', he says, 'is my weight (*pondus meum amor meus*). Whithersoever I am moved, I am moved there by love. By thy gift (*Dono tou* = the Holy Spirit), O Lord, we are set on fire, and are borne aloft; we burn, and we are on the way.'

We climb the ascents that are in the heart... 'With thy fire, with thy good fire, we burn and go on, for we go up to the peace of Jerusalem.' As Thomas Traherne puts it, 'Desire and love/Must in the height of all their rapture move,/Where there is true felicity.'

Not only is our desire God's gift; but its goal, its fulfilment, is also divinely given. As our lesson from the epistle to the Hebrews reminds us, it is because 'we have a great high priest, that is passed into the heavens', that we may 'come boldly unto the throne of grace'. It is through the cross of Christ, our great high priest, that the gates of prayer are truly opened.

We come boldly, with confidence, as friends. As St Thomas remarks, in his meditations on St John 15, Jesus calls his disciples 'friends', and to converse together is the proper condition of friendship.

It is of course a token of the intimacy of divine and human friendship that in the language of prayer, in English, and in many other languages, we are privileged to use the intimate second-person singular pronouns, the 'thee' and 'thou' and 'thine' of intimate friends, rather than the public and formal plurals.

But the theory of Christian prayer would move us even beyond the intimacy of friendship. 'Your life is hid with Christ in

God.' 'I live, yet not I, but Christ in me', says St Paul. We dwell not only in God's presence, as friends, but we dwell in him, and he in us, by grace, and in a profound sense, our prayer is God's prayer in us. 'God's breath in man returning to his birth', as George Herbert puts it. Thus our prayer approaches God not only from outside, as it were, but from within; 'through Jesus Christ our Lord' in the power of the Holy Spirit, that is to say, within the triune Life, within the knowledge and will of God, within the divine providence. Our prayer becomes the free, rational, willing instrument of grace. As Richard Hooker beautifully expresses it:

> For what is the assembling of the Church to learn; but to be the receiving of Angels descended from above? What to pray, but the sending of Angels upwards? His heavenly inspirations and our holy desires are as so many Angels of intercourse and commerce between God and us.

Thus prayer is God's gift to us, God's work in us; our life in God, the redemption of desire. As St Paul explains, all who are in Christ are, by God's grace, converting us, setting straight our loves, transforming, transfiguring; indeed, as Dante says, 'transhumanizing' us. And at this level, when we speak of prayer, we are not speaking just of particular acts of prayer, or occasional prayer, but of prayer as a condition, a direction of life: life lived, that is to say, in continual conversion, continual reference to God. It is that condition of prayer, habitual prayer, that our *Prayer Book*'s system of devotion works to build up in us, and it is really only by such a system of devotion that the condition of habitual prayer can be established in our souls, that our restless hearts 'may surely there be fixed where true joys are to be found'. In that state of being-in-prayer, as John Donne says in one of his sermons,

> … that soule, who, whatsoever string be strucken in her, base or treble, her high or her low estate, is ever tun'd toward God, that soule prayes sometimes when it does not know that it prayes.

In Christ, we are new creatures, born anew, no longer at enmity, but friends of God. We come boldly before the throne of grace. Our reconciliation has been accomplished once and for all; our great high priest has passed into the heavens. But in another sense, our reconciliation is not complete, and will not be complete until we come to know as we are known and love as we are loved.

Prayer reaches out, in faith and hope across that space, and in that reaching out, precisely because it is by faith, trials and tribulations have a necessary place; for the faith must be tried, like precious metal, 'which from the earth is tried, and purified seven times in the fire'.

Ever and again, our desire, as St Ignatius of Antioch puts it, our 'eros is crucified'.

Our loves must be refined and purified. Certainly, the confusions of the world in which we live, the confusions of the Church in which we serve, the confusions within our own souls, present us with manifold trials and temptations.

But all that belongs to our calling, and by the grace of God, who gives manna in the desert and water from the stony rock, we are not without resources. We have a great high priest that has passed into the heavens, Jesus the Son of God. Let us come boldly before the throne of grace, that we may obtain mercy, and find grace to help in time of need. We need only be faithful, we need only hold steadfast in our profession, as our lesson from Hebrews admonishes us. If we, by grace, can just do that, our very trials – indeed, our very sins and failures – will be to us a blessing. As Thomas Traherne puts it, 'Our very rust shall cover us with gold.' Let us then 'come boldly before the throne of grace that we may obtain mercy, and find grace to help in time of need.'

Amen.

HOPE AND TRIBULATION

When these things begin to come to pass, then look up, and lift up your heads; for your redemption draweth nigh.

Our scripture lessons today, from the Revelation of St John the Divine, and from St Luke's Gospel, speak to us of Christian hope and expectation; of the assurance of salvation in the midst of trouble and distress.

'When these things begin to come to pass', says Jesus, 'then look up and lift up your heads, for your redemption draweth nigh'.

The signs of tribulation are the harbingers of glory. 'Behold the fig tree, and all the trees; When they now shoot forth, ye see and know of your own selves that summer is now nigh at hand. So likewise ye, when ye see these things come to pass, know ye that the kingdom of God is nigh at hand.'

Hope and expectation, and the assurance of salvation.

But just what is this hope that arises somehow out of tribulation? What precisely is our Christian expectation?

Our gospel lesson today offers us a dramatic invitation to examine and clarify our thinking on that subject. No doubt all of us have many hopes of various kinds; hopes for ourselves, for our families, and friends; hopes for the Church in which we serve, and for the world in which we live.

Who does not hope for peace, reasonable prosperity, and the resolution of crippling conflicts? Who does not hope for health of mind, and body? For comfort, and security, and opportunity … all such things? Who does not hope for sane, and stable government – in Church and in the nations of the world?

And all these are surely reasonable hopes. And surely there is nothing wrong in hoping for such things. All of them have a legitimate place in our Christian life, and in our prayers. But our gospel lesson today urges us to think more deeply about the substance of our hope, and the meaning of our tribulations, and the relation between hope and tribulation.

Jesus in that gospel lesson reminds us that our worldly hopes, however good, are not enough and can never be enough, because the things of the world are in their very nature passing things. Jesus speaks to us dramatically and urgently about the end, about the end of earthly things.

> There shall be signs in the sun, and in the moon, and in the stars; and upon earth distress of nations, with perplexity, the sea and the waves roaring; men's hearts failing them for fear, and for looking after those things which are coming on the earth: for the powers of heaven shall be shaken. And then shall they see the Son of Man, coming in a cloud with power and great glory.

No doubt when we hear that speech of Jesus it strikes us as a prophecy about the end of time, about some future, almost unimaginable crisis, catastrophe, 'the powers of heaven shall be shaken'. And all down the Christian centuries there have been preachers who have detected the signs of such crisis in their own day. And you know, from time to time, multitudes have gathered on mountaintops to await the end.

But what is Jesus really saying there? What does it mean?

Well, it is of course, a prophecy about the future, about the end of time. But I think it would be a mistake, and a grave mistake, to read it only in a futuristic way. Surely, it has reference also to the present, and speaks of the transitory character of all worldly things, here and now. You see now, now, is the crisis.

'Verily I say unto you, this generation shall not pass away until all be fulfilled.'

For all of us, for each one of us individually, the world must pass away, not just in some vague and unimaginable future, but right now, because worldly things are passing things, and they're passing even as we grasp them in our hands. '*Panta rhei*', said the ancient Greek poet Heraclitus. All things flow, all things are in flux, and no cleverness, no wishful thinking, no advanced technology, can ever make them other than passing things. But it is only through much trouble and distress that we learn the folly of putting our trust in such things. It is only through trouble and distress that we learn the folly of putting our trust in worldly expectations. And it is only through trouble and distress that we learn to find our treasure elsewhere.

When these things begin to come to pass, says Jesus, then look up. Then look up. And find new confidence in the Word of God which does not pass away. 'Heaven and earth shall pass away', says Jesus, 'but my words shall not pass away.'

Our lesson from the Book of Revelation powerfully affirms that gospel exhortation to other-worldliness. Behind St John's vision there lies an experience of tribulation more severe I suppose than any of us has ever known or is ever likely to know. And it is out of the depths of that experience that he speaks.

'Then look up', says the gospel, 'and lift up your heads.' And that's exactly what St John is doing there.

> And I saw a new heaven and a new earth: for the first heaven and the first earth were passed away; and there was no more sea. And I, John, saw the holy city, new Jerusalem, coming down from God out of heaven, prepared as a bride adorned for her husband.

You see, it is in the midst of tribulation and distress, in the midst of the devastation of heaven and earth, that the holy city, the new Jerusalem, the gift of God, descends from God. 'And I heard a great voice out of heaven saying, "Behold, the tabernacle of God is with men, and he will dwell with them . . . and God shall wipe away all tears from their eyes".'

You see, the holy city descends from God, who is Alpha and Omega, the beginning and the end, the first and the last, the living God within whose eternal providence the whole dialectic of hope and tribulation is totally embraced.

You see, He is Alpha and Omega, the beginning and the end, containing, embracing, all things in his knowledge and love. Not the least iota of reality falls outside, not a sparrow falleth. In that eternal knowing, and that eternal loving, which we call providence, even our confusions and stupidities … dare one say, even our sins, have a place? 'For where sin abounded grace did the more abound.' In God's good providence our trials, you see, are never without meaning. 'The trial of your faith worketh patience', says St James in his epistle. 'Let patience have her perfect work, that ye may be perfect and entire.'

All is within the providence of God. And therefore, in the most fundamental sense, 'all is well, and all will be well'.

But if all is within God's providence, if all is indeed 'well', what is the sense of all our struggles and our labours for God's kingdom? Surely it comes as a gift of God, not from our labours.

Remember how St Paul admonishes the Philippians, 'Work out your own salvation in fear and trembling', he says. Then he goes on: 'For it is God that worketh in you both to will and to do his good pleasure.'

See the two sides of that: on the one hand the fearful choices of the human will, undertaken with the utmost seriousness, in fear and trembling. On the other hand, the sure inner workings of the Providence of God. 'It is God that worketh in you both to will and to do his good pleasure.'

It is important to see these two sides, and to see that they are not alternatives.

The religious mind chooses both, says Augustine in *The City of God*. Chooses both, confesses both, maintains both. At that point in *The City of God* in the fifth book, he is debating the position of Cicero, the pagan Cicero, who had argued that to hold a doctrine of providence is surely to evacuate all human initiative and responsibility. Therefore, says Cicero, one must deny the doctrine of providence. You see, he sees providence and human initiative as opposed, as somehow alternatives, as though human action were outside God's providence.

But the point is that all is contained within the providence of God: all our knowings, and all our doings, are within, and not outside. Within God's providence, we have the profound duty of living uncompromisingly, in terms of what truths we know, in terms of what we know of God's truth. And we can do that, and I think we can only do that, in the sure confidence of God's providential care.

Our sure knowledge of God's providence is our assurance

that our labours are not in vain, and our tribulations are not without meaning.

One of our familiar hymns puts it this way:

> When through fiery trials thy pathway shall lie,
> His grace, all-sufficient, shall be thy supply;
> The flame shall not hurt thee; his only design
> Thy dross to consume, and thy gold to refine.

God bless you all and keep you in his grace.

Amen.

Gustave Doré, *Paradiso, 31 Rosa celeste*, ink drawing in Alighieri, Dante. 1892 *The Divine Comedy* by Dante, Illustrated, Complete, London, Cassell and Company, Canto XXXI

What we call the beginning is often the end.
And to make an end is to make a beginning.
The end is where we start from.
T. S. Eliot

THE SUNDAY NEXT BEFORE ADVENT: THE FEAST OF CHRIST THE KING

Jesus said unto his disciples, 'Gather up the fragments that remain, that nothing be lost.'

Today is the last Sunday of the church's year. Next week we shall begin a new year with Advent Sunday; and we shall begin the year in solemn and joyful expectation: 'Behold, thy king cometh unto thee.' 'Hosanna to the Son of David; Blessed is he that cometh.' That's the way the church's year begins, and that's the way the year proceeds. We are made witnesses to the kingship of Jesus: in his life and ministry, in his passion, in his resurrection and enthronement. He calls us, and enables us, by the Spirit's gifts, to seek and find his kingship and his kingdom in our own minds and hearts and lives, here and now, here in our midst. And in that long succession of Sundays after Trinity, the church sets before us, in prayer and scripture lessons, an ordered pattern of spiritual growth, that his kingdom – his kingdom of the Spirit – might be fulfilled in us. 'Thy kingdom come, thy will be done, on earth as it is in heaven.' Thy kingdom come, in us.

Therefore today, as we come to the year's conclusion, it is fitting that we should make a pause, and make a kind of summing up, before we set out upon that road afresh; that we should gather in, as individuals and as a community of believers, the harvest of God's grace, and offer it at the feet of Christ our king.

The Gospel lesson anciently appointed for this Sunday, before the Feast of Christ the King was introduced, actually made the same point. It was St John's account of Jesus feeding the multitudes in the wilderness: the sign of his feeding us with spiritual nutriment in the wilderness of this world. But remember how that story ends: 'When they were filled, he said unto his disciples, "Gather up the fragments that remain, that nothing be lost." Therefore, they gathered them together, and filled twelve baskets with the fragments of the five barley loaves.' The twelve baskets of course stand for the twelve tribes of the new Israel, God's kingdom of the Spirit. Every fragment of spiritual good, all the gifts of God's superabundant grace, are to be gathered in, and treasured in his kingdom: that nothing be lost.

But the kingship of Christ is not easily understood. A strange ambiguity attends the concept through every step of the gospel record, from Bethlehem to Calvary: from King Herod's frantic slaughter of the Innocents to Pilate's nervous question, 'Art thou a king then?' and Jesus' cryptic answer, 'Thou sayest it.' The crowd in Pilate's hall had screamed their hypocritical protest, 'We have no king but Caesar'; but then, finally, upon the cross, the title was inscribed, in Greek, and in Latin, and in Hebrew, for all the world to see, 'Jesus of Nazareth, King of the Jews.'

But what a strange kingship! Who could understand it? Certainly not Herod, and certainly not Pilate; but, you know, even the disciples, even the friends and intimates of Jesus, couldn't understand it. Do you remember that story of James and John, the sons of Zebedee, and the request their mother made of Jesus, that her two sons might sit, one on his right hand,

and the other on his left, in the coming triumph of his kingdom? And remember Jesus' answer: 'The princes of the Gentiles lord it over them, and they that are great exercise authority upon them, but it shall not be so among you.' It shall not be so among you. 'But whosoever will be great among you, let him be your minister; and whosoever will be chief among you, let him be your servant.' His kingship is a kingship of humility and obedience, a conception which turns the worldly standpoint of the disciples upside down.

And think of the accusation against St Paul and his Christian converts in Thessalonica: 'These that have turned the world upside down are come hither also … saying that there is another king, one Jesus.' The Jews and the Roman authorities could see the kingship of Jesus only in terms of worldly power. And all through history, too, many Christians have made exactly that mistake, seeing in Jesus' kingship only the possibility of a better sort of worldliness.

But surely that is not the Gospel, and that is not Jesus' kingship. 'Now is my kingdom not from hence', he says. 'Now is my kingdom not from hence.' He does, indeed, turn the world upside down, but not in the way that Herod or Pilate or the Thessalonian authorities supposed. The ways of his kingdom are much more radical than they could imagine: he turns our whole world, our whole perspective, our whole way of seeing the world and living our lives upside down and inside out.

Blessed, happy, are the strong and prosperous, says the law of worldliness. Blessed are the poor in spirit, those who know their own wretchedness, says Jesus. Blessed are the powerful and forceful, says the world, 'for they get what they go after'. But 'Blessed are the meek and gentle', says the law of Jesus' kingdom, 'they shall inherit the earth'. 'Blessed are those who are full of the world's goods', says the worldly law. 'Blessed are they that hunger and thirst for righteousness', says Jesus, 'for they shall be filled'. 'Blessed are the clever', says the world. 'Blessed are the pure in heart', says Jesus, 'for they shall see God'. 'Blessed are ye when men shall revile and persecute you … for great is your reward in heaven.'

'Whosoever will be great among you', says Jesus, 'let him be your minister, and whosoever will be chief among you, let him be your servant.' The kingship of Jesus is the kingship of a servant, the kingship of humble obedience, and that is the kingship to which he calls all who would follow him. 'Inasmuch as ye have done it unto one of the least of these my brethren ye have done it unto me.'

The signs of Jesus' glory are the signs of his humility, the signs of body broken and blood outpoured: 'He reigns and triumphs from the tree.' That is the strange kingship we venerate, and that is the glory we show forth day by day in the Church's liturgy, as we break the bread and drink the cup. And that is the glory that must adorn our lives if we would truly acknowledge Christ as king. 'Let this mind be in you, which was also in Christ Jesus.' That is the renewal of mind to which the Gospel calls us, that we should follow the example of his great humility and thus become true and faithful citizens of his kingdom. Our Christian year is our witnessing his kingship, and our emulating that kingship in our lives, by his grace. And thus we pray today that he will stir up our wills to set out afresh upon that road, plenteously bringing forth the fruit of good works, and plenteously rewarded, knowing that every fragment of spiritual good is gathered in and treasured up in his kingdom: His kingdom, to whom with the father and the Holy Spirit, one God, be all honour, all glory, and all majesty, now and throughout all ages.

Amen.

NOTES

Father Crouse preached from the ancient Eucharistic Lectionary, that system of Collects, Epistles (or Lessons) and Gospels appointed for the Sunday celebrations of the Holy Eucharist. This doctrinal system received its final form by the seventh century and remained in continuous use in the Western Church, through the tumultuous period of the Reformation, in Roman Catholic, Lutheran, and Anglican churches until the mid-twentieth century. This ancient lectionary has been called 'the most carefully considered and polished treasure of the Western Church' (Common Prayer: Parochial Homilies for the Eucharist, ed. P. Chalmers, E. Eayrs, W. Hankey, Saint Peter Publications, Carlottetown, 1987, 3). The fixed Scripture readings for the feasts of Christ and all the Sundays of the year were the expression of the primitive Church's understanding of pilgrimage and conversion. The doctrinal teaching and logic of this lectionary has been preached and commented on in every age since its inception by theologians, scholars, bishops, and busy pastors. Those who continue to use this ancient Eucharistic lectionary today may be disappointed that the selection of sermons in this volume does not present the carefully ordered systematic thelogy of the second half of the ancient Temporale, but that project will be taken up in a forthcoming third volume of sermons. The present volume of sermons illustrates the outpouring of the Holy Spirit in the Church, the individual Christian soul, and in human institutions, following the first volume of sermons that concluded with Pentecost. This we hope that the sermons here will be of interest and profit for every Christian today, whether or not they worship in a liturgical Church or in a denomination that uses a recently developed multi-year eucharistic lectionary. The first seven sermons of this volume introduce the general logic and organizing principle of the ancient Temporale (the cycle centred of Christ according to the variable date of Easter and fixed date of Christmas) in its two mutually dependent halves. But the Temporale alone is not the Christian Year, and can be interpreted truly only as it continuously intersects, and is in dialogue with, the other major liturgical cycle, the ever-developing Sanctorale: the cycle of the fixed dates of feasts of the saints. The editors believe that this selection of sermons of Robert Crouse from the Sanctorale that highlight sanctification in the individual soul, along with the concluding sermons that focus on institutional sanctification, represent faithfully the spiritual logic of cosmic and person conversion that structures the ancient Temporale and which is the organizing principle of the entire Christian Year, the Temporale and Sancorale.

TRINITY 1/PENTECOST 2, FIRST SERMON
Scripture: 1 John 4:7-21; Luke 16:19-31. Epigraph: 1 John 4:11. Preached unknown.

'O love how deep, how broad', Thomas à Kempis; trans. Benjamin Webb, 'O love how deep, how broad', in *The Book of Common Praise: The Hymn Book of the Anglican Church of Canada* 1938, Toronto: Anglican Book Centre, No. 471.

TRINITY 1/PENTECOST 2, SECOND SERMON
Scripture: 1 John 4:7-21; Luke 16:19-31. Epigraph: 1 John 4:9-11. Preached unknown.

TRINITY 1/PENTECOST 2, AND CORPUS CHRISTI
Scripture: 1 John 4:7-21; Luke 16:19-31. Epigraph: 1 John 4:14-16. Preached 1983, Saint James', Halifax, Nova Scotia.

TRINITY 2/PENTECOST 3
Scripture: 1 John 3:13-24; Luke 14:15-24. Epigraph: 1 John 3:23. Preached 1980, Saint James', Halifax, Nova Scotia.

TRINITY/PENTECOST SEASON AND THE LITURGY
Scripture: 1 Peter 3:8-15; Luke 5:1-11. Epigraph: John 4:23. Preached unknown.

'My God, how wonderful thou art', F.W. Faber, 'My God, how wonderful thou art', in *The Book of Common Praise: The Hymn Book of the Anglican Church of Canada* 1938, Toronto: Anglican Book Centre, No. 370.

'For what is the assembling of the Church to learn', Richard Hooker, *Of the Laws of Ecclesiastical Polity,* 'On Prayer', *Works*, 1977, eds. Edelen and Booty, Cambridge: Belknap, 2nd edition, vol. 1, V.xlviii.2, 201.

TRINITY/PENTECOST SEASON AND MIRACLES
Scripture: II Kings 5:1-17; Luke 17.11-19. Epigraph: Luke 17:19. Preached 2000, All Saints' Church, Wynnwood, PA

'It is by the Lord's mercy ...' , Lamentations 2:22-23.

'In reason's ear they all rejoice', Joseph Addison, 'The spacious firmament on high', in *The Book of Common Praise: The Hymn Book of the Anglican Church of Canada* 1938, Toronto: Anglican Book Centre, No. 602.

'"Art thou he that shall come",' Matthew 11:2-5.

'here we are shown … that it is not only confession of faith', Venerable Bede, *Commentary on the Gospel of Luke* (17:11-19).

'Let us give thanks to our Lord and Saviour', Augustine, *The Sunday Sermons of the Great Fathers, Volume 4* 1996, trans. M.F. Stoal, San Francisco: Ignatius Press, 79.

TRINITY/PENTECOST SEASON AND GLORY
Scripture: Ephesians 4:1-6; Luke 14:1-11. Epigraph: Luke 14:10. Preached 1979, King's College Chapel, Halifax, Nova Scotia.

'Grace has five effects in us …', Aquinas, *Summa Theologica* Part II of Part I, Q. 111, trans, Fathers of the English Dominican Province https://www.newadvent.org/summa/2111.htm

CONCEPTION OF THE BLESSED VIRGIN MARY
Commemoration: 8 December. Scripture: Acts 1.12-14; Luke 1.39-49. Epigraph: Luke 1:28. Preached 1978, King's College Chapel, Halifax, Nova Scotia.

Papal Bull, 'Ineffabilis Deus', Pope Pius IX, 1854: https://www.papalencyclicals.net/pius09/p9ineff.htm

'The union of both natures … ', Anthony Stafford, *The Femall Glory: the Life and Death of the Blessed Virgin: together with the Apology of the Author, and an Essay on the Cultus of the Blessed Virgin Mary*, ed. Orby Shipley, 4th ed. 1869, London: Longmans, Green, Reader, and Dyer, lxxxix-xc.

'Salvation to all that will is nigh …', John Donne, '*La Corona: Annunciation*', 1967, in *Complete Poetry and Selected Prose*, ed. John Hayward, London: The Nonesuch Press, 276.

THE ANNUNCIATION OF THE BLESSED VIRGIN MARY, FIRST SERMON

Commemoration: 25 March. Scripture: Isaiah 7:10-15; Luke 1:26-38. Epigraph: Isaiah 45:8. Preached 1976, King's College Chapel, Halifax, Nova Scotia.

'The wind blows where it will …', John 3:8.

'No! I am not Prince Hamlet; nor was meant to be …', T.S. Eliot, 'The Love Song of J. Alfred Prufrock', 1954, in *Selected Poems*, London: Faber & Faber, line 111.

'Rise up, my love, my fair one, and come away.' Song of Songs 2:10-13.

THE ANNUNCIATION OF THE BLESSED VIRGIN MARY, SECOND SERMON

Commemoration: 25 March. Scripture: Isaiah 7:10-15; Luke 1:26-38. Epigraph: Isaiah 45:8. Preached 1998, King's College Chapel, Halifax, Nova Scotia.

'As the rain cometh down …', Isaiah 55:10-11.

'No one is like her … ', Romano Guardini, *The Rosary of Our Lady,* 1955, New York: P.J. Kennedy and Sons, 37.

THE FALLING ASLEEP OF THE BLESSED VIRGIN MARY

Commemoration: 15 August. Scripture: Acts 1.12-14; Luke 1.39-49. Epigraph: Judith 13:22-23. Preached unknown.

ST JOSEPH OF NAZARETH

Commemoration: 19 March. Scripture: Isaiah 9:2-7; Luke 2:15-21. Epigraph: Matthew 1:16. Preached 1981, King's College Chapel, Halifax, Nova Scotia.

'One saith unto him, Behold …', Matthew 12:47-50.

'*Gratia non tollit naturam, sed perfecit.*' (Grace does not destroy nature, but perfects it.) Thomas Aquinas, *Summa Theologiae,* I, I, 8 ad 2.1, 1920, trans. Fathers of the English Dominican Province, https://www.newadvent.org/summa/

THE NATIVITY OF ST JOHN THE BAPTIST
Commemoration: 24 June. Scripture: Isaiah 40:1-11; Luke 1:57-80. Epigraph: Matthew 11:9-10. Preached 2001, Saint Mary's, Crousetown, Nova Scotia.

'For giving me desire', Thomas Traherne, 'Desire', in *The Oxford Book of Christian Verse*, 1973, ed. Lord David Cecil, Oxford: Clarendon Press, no. 201, 272.

ST ANDREW
Commemoration: 30 November. Scripture: Romans 10.8-18; Matthew 4.18-20. Epigraph: Revelation 21:14. Preached unknown.

'Twelve poor men, by Christ anointed', Athelstan Riley, 'Saints of God! Lo, Jesus' People', in *The Book of Common Praise: The Hymn Book of the Anglican Church of Canada* 1938, Toronto: Anglican Book Centre, No. 200.

ST PHILIP AND ST JAMES THE APOSTLES WITH ST JAMES THE BROTHER OF THE LORD
Commemoration: 1 May. Scripture: James 1:1-12; John 14:1-14. Epigraph: John 14:8-9. Preached unknown.

'God's presence and his very self', John Henry Newman, 'Praise to the Holiest in the height', in *The Book of Common Praise: The Hymn Book of the Anglican Church of Canada* 1938, Toronto: Anglican Book Centre, No. 384.

ST MATTHEW

Commemoration: 21 September. Scripture: 2 Corinthians 4:1-6; Matthew 9:9-13. Epigraph: Matthew 9:9. Preached 1987, King's College Chapel, Halifax, Nova Scotia.

Caravaggio, *The Calling of Saint Matthew*, c.1599-1600, San Luigi dei Francesi, Rome.

'That light doth so transform', Dante Alighieri, *Paradise* 1962, trans. Sayers and Reynolds, London: Penguin Books, XXXIII, 100-105.

Crouse says: 'As St Thomas remarks, in his "Lectures on St Matthew": 'It is objected that this cannot be, that at one word he arose and followed him'.'

'God moves in free beings ...', Aquinas. Here Crouse appears to be paraphrasing *Summa Theologica* Q. 44. See https://www.ccel.org/ccel/aquinas/summa.TP_Q44_A3.html

ST PETER

Commemoration: 29 June. Scripture: 1 Peter 1:1-9; Matthew 16:13-19. Epigraph: Luke 22:31-32. Preached unknown.

ST JAMES, APOSTLE AND MARTYR

Commemoration: 25 July. Scripture: Acts 11.27-12:3; Mark 10:32-40. Epigraph: Ephesians 2:20. Preached 1988, Saint James', Bridgetown, Nova Scotia.

TRANSFIGURATION

Commemoration: 6 August. Scripture: 2 Peter 1:16-21; Matthew 17:1-9. Epigraph: 2 Peter 1:16. Preached 2000, Saint Mary's, Crousetown, Nova Scotia.

'The heavens declare the glory of the Lord ...', Psalm 19:1-5.

'And the glory of the Lord abode …', Exodus 24:16-17.

'My God, how wonderful thou art', F.W. Faber, 'My God, how wonderful thou art', in *The Book of Common Praise: The Hymn Book of the Anglican Church of Canada* 1938, Toronto: Anglican Book Centre, No. 370.

ST LUKE

Commemoration: 18 October. Scripture: 2 Tim 4.5-13; Luke 24.44-53. Epigraph: Job 13:15. Preached 1998, Saint Alban's Cathedral, Prince Albert, Saskatchewan.

'Lord, it belongs not …', Richard Baxter, 'Lord, it belongs not to my care', in *The Book of Common Praise: The Hymn Book of the Anglican Church of Canada* 1938, Toronto: Anglican Book Centre, No. 662.

ST MARY MAGDALENE

Commemoration: 22 July. Scripture: Acts 13:27-31; John 20.11-18. Epigraph: 1 Peter 4:8. Preached Unknown.

'It will be said on that day …', Isaiah 25:9.

THE CONVERSION OF ST PAUL

Commemoration: 25 January. Scripture: Acts 21:40-22:16; Luke 21:10-19. Epigraph: Galatians 2:20. Preached 1982, King's College Chapel, Halifax, Nova Scotia.

ST MICHAEL AND ALL ANGELS, FIRST SERMON

Commemoration: 29 September. Scripture: Revelation 12:7-11; Matthew 18:1-10. Epigraph: Ps. 91:11. Preached 1978, King's College Chapel, Halifax, Nova Scotia.

'the angels represent the operations of divine providence', Sayers and Reynolds, Notes, Dante, 'Paradise Canto XXVIII', London: Penguin Classics, 1962.

'God, which moveth mere natural agents as an efficient (cause) only …' , Richard Hooker, *Laws of Ecclesiastical Polity in Modern English,* ed. Littlejohn et al., 2019, Lincoln: Davenant Institute, Vol I. Book I, Chapter 4, 59.

'Not where the wheeling systems darken', Francis Thompson, 'In No Strange Land', in *The Selected Poems of Francis Thompson* 1907, London: Methuen and Co. Ltd, 172.

ST MICHAEL AND ALL ANGELS, SECOND SERMON
Commemoration: 29 September. Scripture: Revelation 12:7-11; Matthew 18:1-10. Epigraph: Matthew 18:3. Preached 1989, King's College Chapel, Halifax, Nova Scotia.

'Thick as sparks from molten iron …', Dante Alighieri, *Paradise*, trans. Laurence Binyon in The Portable Dante, 1947, ed. Pablo Milano, New York, Viking Press, XXVII, 89-90; 94-96.

ST CLEMENT OF ROME
Born: c. 35. Commemoration: 23 November. Scripture: 1 Peter 5:1-4; Matthew 16:13-19. Epigraph: 1 Corinthians 14:26, 33. Preached 1981, King's College Chapel, Halifax, Nova Scotia.

'Since all this is clear … ', Clement of Rome, *The Epistle of Saint Clement*, 1915, ed. John A. F. Gregg, London: Society for Promoting Christian Knowledge, XL-XLI, 54-55.

'Grace does not destroy nature … ', Saint Thomas Aquinas, *Summa Theologiae,* I, I, 8 ad 2. 1.

ST CLEMENT OF ALEXANDRIA
Born: 150. Commemoration: 4 December. Scripture: Daniel 2:17-24; Matthew 13:9-17. Epigraph: Daniel 2:24. Preached 1997, location unknown.

ST CECILIA

Born: c. 200. Commemoration: 22 November. Scripture: Hosea 2:16b,17b, 21-22; Matthew 25:1-13. Epigraph: Job 38:6-7. Preached 1984, King's College Chapel, Halifax, Nova Scotia.

'Such musick (as 'tis said)', John Milton, 'Ode on the Morning of Christ's Nativity', in *Milton's Ode on the Morning of Christ's Nativity,* 1891, Cambridge: University Press, 1-13.

'As from the power of sacred lays', 'A Song For St Cecilia's Day', in *The Poems of John Dryden,* 1913, ed. John Sargeaunt. London: Oxford University Press, 1913, 197.

ST HILARY OF POITIERS

Born: c. 310. Commemoration: 13 January. Scripture: 1 John 2:18-25; Luke 12:8-12. Epigraph: Psalm 37:30. Preached 1983, King's College Chapel, Halifax, Nova Scotia.

'If the Word was truly made flesh', and 'Preserve, I pray thee, undefiled, this religion', Hilary of Poitiers, *De Trinitate, Hilarii Pictaviensis De Trinitate*: 1903, bibliothecae ser V. Romae: Foranzi et Socii.

ST JOHN CHRYSOSTOM

Born: c. 347. Commemoration: 27 January. Scripture Lessons: Daniel 2:17-24; Matthew 13:9-17. Epigraph: Matthew 13:11. Preached 1981, King's College Chapel, Halifax, Nova Scotia.

'Although he struggled, according to the precepts … ', Edward Gibbon, *The History of the decline and fall of the Roman Empire* Vol. 3, 5th ed., 1912, ed. J.B. Bury, London: Methuen & Co., 374-376.

'From this story, G. L. Prestige draws the very Anglican moral …', Crouse refers here to the Chaplain of New College, Oxford and author of influential texts on patristics, G.L. Prestige (1889-1955).

'If you live alone … ', Basil the Great, *Questions of the Brothers,* 2014, ed. Anna M. Silvas, Leiden: Brill, 79.

'plain how Heav'n is everywhere', Dante Alighieri, *Paradise*, 1962, trans. Sayers and Reynolds, London: Penguin Books, 88-90.

THE EXALTATION OF THE HOLY CROSS
Commemoration: 14 September. Scripture: Hebrews 9:11-15; Matthew 20:20-28. Epigraph: John 12:31-33. Preached 1988, King's College Chapel, Halifax, Nova Scotia.

'Pilgrimage of Aetheria', Also known as the *Itinerarium Egeriae, Diary of a Pilgrimage,* 2002 trans. George E. Gingras, New York: Paulist Press.

'The Royal Banners forward go', and 'O Tree of glory, Tree most fair', Venantius Fortunatus, 'The Royal Banners forward go', and 'O Tree of glory, Tree most fair', trans. Percy Dearmer, in *The Book of Common Praise: The Hymn Book of the Anglican Church of Canada* 1938, Toronto: Anglican Book Centre, Nos. 128 & 129.

ST AUGUSTINE
Born: 354. Commemoration: 28 August. Scripture: Hebrews 12:22; John 14:5-15. Epigraph: Romans 12:2. Preached 1986, Saint Augustine's, The Forties, Nova Scotia.

'*Tolle, lege* … ', Augustine, *Confessions*, 1961, trans. R. S. Pine-Coffin, London: Penguin, VIII.xii.29.

'By its own weight, a body inclines to its own place', Augustine, *Confessions*, 1961, trans. R. S. Pine-Coffin, London: Penguin, XIII.ix.10.

ST DENYS AND ROBERT GROSSETESTE
St Denys Born: First or fifth century. Commemoration: 9 October.

Robert Grossteste Born: c. 1168. Commemoration: 9 October. Epigraph: James 1:17. Preached 2003, King's College Chapel, Halifax, Nova Scotia. Scripture: Daniel 2:17-24; Matthew 13:9-17.

'Every good gift, ...', James 1:17. Dionysius the Areopagite (St Denys) begins his entire corpus with a brief commentary on this passage.

'When God crowns the merits of the saints ...', Saint Augustine, 'Grace and Free Will', in *The Teacher, The Free Choice of the Will, Grace and Free Will*, 1968, trans. Robert P. Russell, Washington: Catholic University of America Press, 6.15, 267.

Hilduin of Saint-Denis, 'The Prose *Passio S Dionysii*', in *Prose and Verse*, 2017, ed. and trans. Michael Lapidge, Leiden: Brill, 229-303.

See Plato's Allegory of the Sun. Plato, *Republic*, 506d-509c.
See Dante's ninth heaven, *Paradise*, XXVIII.

'TRINITY!...' Pseudo-Dionysius, 'The Mystical Theology', in *Pseudo-Dionysius: The Complete Works*, 1987, trans. Colm Luibhead, New York: Paulist Press, 135.

ST BENEDICT
Born: 480. Commemoration: 21 March. Scripture: Hebrews 11:13-16; 12:1-2; John 4:32-38. Epigraph: Hebrews 11:14. Preached 1979, King's College Chapel, Halifax, Nova Scotia.

'Full of ignorant learning', Gregory the Great, *Life and Miracles of Saint Benedict*, Book Two of the Dialogues, 1949, trans. Odo J. Zimmerman and Benedict R. Avery, Collegeville: Saint John's Abbey Press, 2.

'The Reverend Father wrote a Rule for monks ...', Gregory the Great, *Life and Miracles of Saint Benedict,* Book Two of the Dialogues,

1949, trans. Odo J. Zimmerman and Benedict R. Avery, Collegeville: Saint John's Abbey Press, 74.

ST BENEDICT AND ARCHBISHOP CRANMER

Cranmer Born: 1489. Commemoration: 21 March. Scripture: Hebrews 11:13-16; 12:1-2; John 4:32-38. Epigraph: Hebrews 11: 16. Preached 1996, King's College Chapel, Halifax, Nova Scotia.

'*scienter nescius, et sapienter indoctus*', Gregory the Great, *Life of Saint Benedict,* 1898, London: Thomas Baker, Christian Classics Ethereal Library Print Basis, URL: http://www.ccel.org/ccel/gregory/life_rule.html.

'plastered like swallows' nests against the cliff', Pius II, *Commentaries,* 2018, trans. Meserve, Vol. 3, Book VI, chapter 21, paragraph 5, 321. Pius II explains that Benedict 'made his bed on the hard stone. Here he mortified his flesh with vigils and fasting; here he offered his service to God. Disciples followed him and began to inhabit the cave. Just as swallows build their nests into clefts in the rock of a high cliff, so this monastery clings to its towering crag, even as fragments of rock tumble down which kill the monks or carry away parts of the building.'

'threshold of paradise' Petrarch said of Sacro Speco, the sacred cave where Benedict lived before founding Monte Cassino in 529, '*Illud immane sed devotum specus quod qui viderunt, vidisse qodammodo paradisi limen credunt.*' 'Those who saw the impressing but holy caves believe to have seen the threshold to paradise', Francesco Petrarch, *De vita solitaria,* II, 9.

ST GREGORY THE GREAT

Born: 540. Commemoration: 12 March. Scripture: Daniel 2:17-24; Matthew 4:13-24. Epigraph: Matthew 13:11. Preached 1992, King's College Chapel, Halifax, Nova Scotia.

'had no idea of building up a new social order', Christopher Dawson, *The Making of Europe: An Introduction to the History of European Unity,* 1945, New York: Sheed & Ward, 192.

'In a straitened age ... ', Inscription by Pope John III in the Church of the Most Holy Apostles, quoted in Christopher Dawson, *The Making of Europe: An Introduction to the History of European Unity,* 1945, New York: Sheed & Ward, 174.

'fastened with the cable of an anchor ...', Bede, *Ecclesiastical History of the English Nation*, 1962, trans. J. E. King, Cambridge, Massachusetts: Harvard University Press, 189.

'... founded a school of singers', John the Deacon, *Life of Gregory,* quoted in Henry Wall, *A Dictionary of Christian Biography and Literature at the end of the Sixth Century,* 1911, John Murray, 908.

'Wherever you go, let the pastoral book ....', Johannes Quasten, ed. *Ancient Christian Writers: The Works of the Fathers in Translation, Saint Gregory the Great: Pastoral Care*, 1950 trans. Henry Davis, Mahwah: Paulist Press, 13.

'When a preacher cries aloud ...', Johannes Quasten, ed. *Ancient Christian Writers: The Works of the Fathers in Translation, Saint Gregory the Great: Pastoral Care*, 1950 trans. Henry Davis, Mahwah: Paulist Press, 201-202.

ST JOHN OF DAMASCUS
Born: c. 645. Commemoration: 4 December. Epigraph: Job 13.15. Preached unknown.

'Tell us, Poet, what it is you do', Rainer Maria Rilke. This poem was written in 1921, a year before *Sonnets to Orpheus*. We have not found this translation in print, and it may be Fr Crouse's free translation.

'Only he who has raised the lyre … 'Rainer Maria Rilke, *Sonnets to Orpheus* 2015, trans. A. Saint Kline, London: Poetry in Translation, I.9.

ST HENRY OF FINLAND

Born: 1100. Commemoration: 20 January. Epigraph: Matthew 4:15-16. Preached unknown.

'New machinery and, adaptations and adjustments…', Evelyn Underhill, *The Parish Priest and the Life of Prayer*, 1937, London: Mowbray, 5-6.

'Be purified, and you shall be clean ….', Gregory Nazianzen, 'Oration on the Holy Lights', trans. Charles Gordon Browne and James Edward Swallow, in *Nicene and Post-Nicene Fathers, Second Series,* Vol. 7, 1894 eds. Philip Schaff and Henry Wace, Buffalo, NY: Christian Literature Publishing Co. 359.

ST FRANCIS OF ASSISI

Born: c. 1181. Commemoration: 4 October. Epigraph: Galatians 6:14. Preached 1984, King's College Chapel, Halifax, Nova Scotia.

'All creatures of our God and King', W.H. Draper, based on Saint Francis of Assisi, 'All creatures of our God and King', in *The Book of Common Praise: The Hymn Book of the Anglican Church of Canada* 1938, Toronto: Anglican Book Centre, No. 399.

ST THOMAS AQUINAS, FIRST SERMON

Born: c. 1225. Commemoration: 28 January. Epigraph: Wisdom of Solomon 3:7. Preached 1977 location unknown.

'The study of philosophy does not mean to learn what others have thought, but to learn what is the truth of things.' Crouse quotes Aquinas here, but adds that this comment is directed at Siger of Brabant. The text from Aquinas' *Commentaria in Aristotelis De Caelo et Mundo* reads:

Now, some claim that these poets and philosophers, and especially Plato, did not understand these matters in the way their words sound on the surface, but wished to conceal their wisdom under certain fables and enigmatic statements. Moreover, they claim that Aristotle's custom in many cases was not to object against their understanding, which was sound, but against their words, lest anyone should fall into error on account of their way of speaking. So says Simplicius in his Commentary. But Alexander held that Plato and the other early philosophers understood the matter just as the words sound literally, and that Aristotle undertook to argue not only against their words but against their understanding as well. Whichever of these may be the case, it is of little concern to us, because the study of philosophy aims not at knowing what men feel, but at what is the truth of things. (Paragraph 227, Lecture 22: 'Whether the universe is infinite by eternal duration.' Aquinas, *In De caelo*, trans. Larcher and Conway, lib. 1 l. 22 n. 8. https://isidore.co/peras/peras/DeCoelo.htm)

ST THOMAS AQUINAS, SECOND SERMON

Epigraph: Wisdom of Solomon: 6:17-20. Preached 1983, King's College Chapel, Halifax, Nova Scotia.

'These three run together …', *Summa Theologica* ia-2ae. Iv. 3 *Saint Thomas Aquinas, Philosophical Texts,* 1955, trans T .G. G. Cumberlege, Oxford: Oxford University Press.

'this strange disease of modern life …', Matthew Arnold, 'The Scholar

Gypsy', *The Poems of Matthew Arnold, 1840-1867*, 1913, London, Oxford University Press, 203-4.

'Not merely gathering information about divine things ...', Aquinas, 916, 957 Opus c. Xiv, *Exposition, de Divinis Nominibus*, ii, lect. 4.

'*ut cantando moreretur et moriendo cantaret* ...' This is inscribed at the site of Aquinas' first burial, at Fossanova. https://thomistica.net/st-thomas-last-days

ALL SAINTS
Commemoration: 1 November. Scripture: Revelation 7:9-17; Matthew 5:1-12. Epigraph: Ephesians. 4:4-7. Preached 1982, Saint James', Halifax, Nova Scotia.

Collect in the *Book of Common Prayer, Canada,* 1962, Toronto: Anglican Book Centre, 299:

O ALMIGHTY God, who hast knit together thine elect in one communion and fellowship, in the mystical body of thy Son Christ our Lord: Grant us grace so to follow thy blessed Saints in all virtuous and godly living, that we may come to those unspeakable joys, which thou hast prepared for them that unfeignedly love thee; through Jesus Christ our Lord. Amen.

ALL SAINTS/ALL SOULS
Commemorations: 1 & 2 November. Scripture: Revelation 7:9-17; Matthew 5:1-12. Epigraph: Matthew 5:8. Preached 2004, All Souls' Church, Oklahoma City.

'Lift your eyes, ye sons of light', John Cennick, 'Children of the heavenly King', in *The Book of Common Praise: The Hymn Book of the Anglican Church of Canada* 1938, Toronto: Anglican Book Centre, No. 413.

'heavenly avarice', Thomas Traherne, in 'Desire', *Oxford Book of Christian Verse*, 1951, ed. Lord David Cecil, Oxford: Clarendon Press, no. 201, 272.

'Therefore I say, that not only … ', Dante Alighieri, *Convivio*, Tutte le pera, 1981, ed. L. Blasucci, Florence: IV.12, 176-177.

'Now in the meantime, … ', Peter Abelard, 'O what their joy and their glory must be', trans. J. M. Neale, in *The Book of Common Praise: The Hymn Book of the Anglican Church of Canada* 1938, Toronto: Anglican Book Centre, No. 613.

ALL SOULS
Commemoration: 2 November. Scripture: Wisdom 3:1-9; 1 Thessalonians 4:13-18; John 5:24-27. Epigraph: Philippians 2:12-13. Preached 1980, King's College Chapel, Halifax, Nova Scotia.

'*Dies irae*' is a Latin hymn sequence sung before the proclamation of the gospel on All Souls' Day, describing the trumpet summoning souls before the throne of God at the Last Judgement. It is commonly attributed to Thomas of Celano (1200-1265), though it is possibly much older. The chant is characterized by its accentual stress, rhymed lines, and trochaic metre.

'Weeping o're the grave, we make our song', 'Kontakion of the Departed', W. J. Birbeck trans., in *The Book of Common Praise: The Hymn Book of the Anglican Church of Canada* 2000, Toronto: Anglican Book Centre, No. 350.

HARVEST
Scripture: Isaiah 55:1-12; John 6:27-35. Epigraph: Isaiah 55: 10-11. Preached 1976, King's College Chapel, Halifax, Nova Scotia.
'Bare ruined choirs', William Shakespeare, *Sonnet 73*, line 4.

MARRIAGE, FIRST SERMON

Scripture: Galatians 5:16-24; Luke 10:25-37. Epigraph: Luke 10:28. Preached 1977, All Souls' Chapel, Saint Peter's Cathedral, Charlottetown, Prince Edward Island.

MARRIAGE, SECOND SERMON

Scripture: John 2:1-11. Epigraph: John 2:11. Preached 1980, Saint Thomas Aquinas, Halifax.

'Marriage is a school and exercise of virtue …', Jeremy Taylor, 'The Marriage Ring', in *Selected English Sermons,* 1939, ed. Hensley Henson, London: Oxford University Press, H. Milford, 132.

THE ORDERING OF DEACONS

Scripture: 1 Timothy 3:8-13; Luke 12:35-38. Epigraph: Isaiah 55:10, 11. Preached 1981, Saint James', Halifax, Nova Scotia.

'Yea angels tremble when they see', trans. Neale in *The Book of Common Praise: The Hymn Book of the Anglican Church of Canada* 1938, Toronto: Anglican Book Centre, No. 23.

'It is the mark of God's omnipotent goodness', says Saint Thomas Aquinas …' *Summa Theologica,* Q. 49 in *Saint Thomas Aquinas, Philosophical Texts,* 1955, trans T. G. G. Cumberlege, Oxford: Oxford University Press.

'Yet sweet to us appears …', Dante Alighieri, *Paradise,* 1962, trans. Sayers and Reynolds, London: Penguin Books, XXIV, 4ff.

THE ORDINATION OF A PRIEST

Scripture: Isaiah 55:10-12; Ephesians 4:7-13; John 10:1-16. Epigraph: Isaiah 55:11. Preached 1980, Saint Peter's, Charlottetown, Prince Edward Island.

'One offering single and complete', William Bright, 'Once, only once, and once for all' in *The Book of Common Praise: The Hymn Book of the Anglican Church of Canada* 1938, Toronto: Anglican Book Centre, No. 241.

THE CONSECRATION OF A BISHOP
Scripture: 1 Timothy 3:1-7; John 21:15-17. Epigraph: John 21:16. Preached 1993, Saint John the Baptist, North Sydney, Nova Scotia.

'Gregory did his great work ...', F. Holmes Dudden, *Gregory the Great: His Place in History and thought, Volume I*, 2004, Eugene: Wipf and Stock, 281.

'In the midst of the unsteady flow of time ...', Gregory, *Moralia in Job*, xxxi, 28, 55, as quoted in *Robert Austin Markus, Gregory the Great and His World,* 1997, Cambridge: Cambridge University Press, 3.

INDUCTION OF A RECTOR
Scripture: Luke 10:38-42. Epigraph: Luke 10:42. Preached 1975, Saint James', Halifax, Nova Scotia.

'In that abyss I saw ...', Dante Alighieri, *Paradise*, 1962, trans. Sayers and Reynolds, London: Penguin Books, XXXIII, 85-87; 103-105.

A THANKSGIVING FOR RESTORATION OF A CHURCH BUILDING
Epigraph: Psalms 84:1-2. Preached June 2, 1997, Saint George's, Halifax, Nova Scotia.

'Hallowed this dwelling ...', from 'Only-begotten, Word of God eternal', trans. M. J. Blacker, in *The Book of Common Praise: The Hymn Book of the Anglican Church of Canada,* 1938, Toronto: Anglican Book Centre, No. 346.

'Bright is the noble work …', Abbot Suger of Saint Denis, *Abbot Suger on the Abbey Church of Saint-Denis and its Art Treasures*, 1946, ed. and trans. Erwin Panofsky, Princeton: Princeton University Press, 47-48.

'one thing I have desired', Psalm 27:4.

THE UNIVERSITY AND THE SPIRIT
Scripture: Galatians 5:16-24; Luke 10:25-37. Epigraph: Galatians 5:16. Preached 1998, King's College Chapel, Halifax, Nova Scotia.

A UNIVERSITY MATRICULATION SERVICE
Scripture: Ephesians 5:15-21; Matthew 22:1-14. Epigraph: Proverbs 9:1. Preached 1994, King's College Chapel, Halifax, Nova Scotia.

THE UNIVERSITY AND THE TRANSFIGURATION
Scripture: 2 Peter 1:16-21; Matthew 17:1-9. Epigraph: Galatians 5:16. Preached 1989, King's College Chapel, Halifax, Nova Scotia.

'The object of a university …', Edward Pusey as quoted in Henry Parry Liddon (1893-1897), *Life of Edward Bouverie Pusey: Doctor of Divinity, Canon of Church: Regius Professor of Hebrew in the University of Oxford*, 1894, ed. J. O. Johnston and Robert J. Wilson, vol 3, London: Longmans, Green, 390.

'The College must possess to a very great extent …', W. B. King … Unknown.

A UNIVERSITY BACCALAUREATE SERVICE
Scripture: 1 Corinthians 1-13; Luke 18:31-43. Epigraph: 1 Corinthians 13:9. Preached 1982, King's College Chapel, Halifax, Nova Scotia.

'All men by nature desire to know', Aristotle, *Metaphysics*, I.1 (980a 21) *Basic Works of Aristotle*, ed. and trans. Richard McKeon, 2001, New York: Penguin.

'The Philosopher' = Aristotle

sub specie aeternitatis = under the aspect of eternity.

'Where the gods dwell forever in perfect peace ...', this is not a quote, but a paraphrase in the spirit of Homer, *Odyssey*, VI.42-6.

'life of the gods ... life too high for humans', Aristotle, *Nicomachean Ethics*, X, 7 (1177b 25) in *Basic Works of Aristotle*, 2001, ed. and trans. Richard McKeon, New York: Penguin.

'whether some other doctrine is required ...', Saint Thomas Aquinas, *Summa Theologica*, I, q. 1, a. 1.

'In that abyss I saw ... ', Dante Alighieri, *Paradise*, 1962, trans. Sayers and Reynolds, London: Penguin Books, XXXIII, 85-87; 103-105.

'*regina artium*' = 'Queen of the arts.'

A SERMON ON PRAYER

Scripture: Zechariah 1:18-2:13; Hebrews 4:14-5:10. Epigraph: Hebrews 4:14-16. Preached 1995, King's College Chapel, Halifax, Nova Scotia.

'Desire itself prays ...', Augustine, Sermon LXXX, 7, *PL*, 38, 497; cf. A. Cacciari, Saint Agostino d'Ippona. La preghiera. Epistola 130 a Proba (Rome, 1981), 48.

'... desire has the force of prayer ... ', Aquinas, '*Unde et oratio est petitio decentium a Deo, et ideo desiderium habet vim orationis*' – this latter line ('*desiderium habet vim orationis*') Crouse translates as 'desire has the force of prayer ...', in English context, see: *Saint Thomas Aquinas Commentary on 1 Thessalonians 5:2*. 1969, trans. Michael Duffy, Albany: Magi Books. https://isidore.co/aquinas/english/SS1Thes.htm

'Every good and holy desire …', Richard Hooker, *Laws of Ecclesiastical Polity*, Works, 2nd edition, 1841, ed. John Keble, vol. 1, V.xlviii.2, 201.

'It is thou, O God', Augustine, *Confessions,* Book I. i (1), trans. Robert Crouse.

'My love is my weight', Augustine, *Confessions,* Book XIII. ix (10), trans. Robert Crouse.

'Desire and love …', Thomas Traherne, 'Contentment is a Sleepy Thing', *Oxford Book of Christian Verse*, 1951, ed. Lord David Cecil, Oxford: Clarendon Press, no. 209, 291.

'Jesus calls his disciples "friends"', *Saint Thomas Aquinas commentary on John XV Lecture 3*, 1998, trans. Fabian R. Larcher, Albany: Magi Books, 1998. https://isidore.co/aquinas/english/John15.htm

'God's breath in man returning to his birth', George Herbert, 'Prayer', in *The Oxford Book of Christian Verse*, 1951, ed. Lord David Cecil, Oxford: Clarendon Press, no. 106, 139.

'For what is the assembling of the Church …', Richard Hooker, *Laws of Ecclesiastical Polity,* in *Works,* 2nd edition, 1841, John Keble, vol. 1, V.xxiii, 115.

'That soule, who whatever …', John Donne, 'Preached Upon Candlemas Day', in *The Sermons of John Donne,* Vol. IV, 1962, ed. Evelyn M. Simpson and George R. Potter, Berkeley: University of California Press, Vol. 4, no. 12, 310.

'… our eros is crucified', Ignatius of Antioch, 'Letter to the Romans', in *The Early Church Fathers and Other Works,* 1953, ed. and trans. Cyril Richardson, Philadelphia: The Westminster Press, paragraph 7, 92.

'Our very rust shall cover us ...', Thomas Traherne, 'Christian Ethics', *The Oxford Book of Christian Verse*, 1973, ed. Lord David Cecil, Oxford: Clarendon Press, no. 207, 286.

HOPE AND TRIBULATION

Scripture: Revelation 21:1-14; Luke 21:25-33. Epigraph: Luke 21:28. Preached 2002, Saint John's, Vancouver, British Columbia.

'*Panta rhei*', 'all things flow', Heraclitus, *Fragments* 12, 49, 91.

'all is well, and all ...', Julian of Norwich (1342-1416), 'All shall be well, and all shall be well, and all manner of things shall be well', *Revelations of Divine Love,* 2015, trans. Barry Windeatt, Oxford: Oxford World Classics, Ch 27, 74.

Augustine, *The City of God Books* I-VII, 1950, ed. E. Gilson, trans. Zema and Walsh, Washington: Catholic University of America Press, 258.

'When through fiery trials thy pathway shall lie ...', George Keith, 1787, 'How firm a foundation', in *The Book of Common Praise: The Hymn Book of the Anglican Church of Canada* 1938, Toronto: Anglican Book Centre, No. 499.

'What we call the beginning...', *Four Quartets*, 'Little Gidding' V, London: Faber and Faber, 1 - 3. Printed with permission.

THE SUNDAY NEXT BEFORE ADVENT: THE FEAST OF CHRIST THE KING

Scripture: Jeremiah 23:5-8; John 1:35-45. Epigraph: John 6:12. Preached 1999, All Saints, Oklahoma City.

'He reigns and triumphs from the tree', Fortunatus, 'The Royal Banners Forward Go', trans. Percy Dearmer, in *The Book of Common*

Praise: The Hymn Book of the Anglican Church of Canada 1938, Toronto: Anglican Book Centre, No.128.

'… we pray today that he will stir up our wills', Collect for Sunday Next Before Advent: 'Stir up, we beseech thee, O Lord, the wills of thy faithful people; that they, plenteously bringing forth the fruit of good works, may of thee be plenteously rewarded; through Jesus Christ our Lord', in *Book of Common Prayer,* Canada, 1962, Toronto: Anglican Book Centre, 259.

LIST OF ILLUSTRATIONS

FRONTISPIECE

Anon., *Cosmic Christ* tympanum, stone sculpture, c. 1130 (Sainte Marie Madeleine de Vézelay, Burgundy, France). Photo: Gerd Eichmann, 20 September 2008. https://upload.wikimedia.org/wikipedia/commons/1/12/V%C3%A9zelay-Sainte-Marie-Madeleine-122-Tympanon_innen-2008-gje.jpg

TIMELINE, pp. 20-21

Timeline graphic design: Morgan Rogers, co & co, Halifax, N.S.

NASA and the Space Telescope Science Institute, *Star Dying*, Webb Space Telescope photograph, March 14, 2023 (Sun's orbit), https://webbtelescope.org/contents/media/images/2023/111/01GTWASGERK0M8G86WZZSRC1ZX?fbclid=IwAR0wQW-Hge-FsRjWMTttki3IlfydYX6iKpVx2HwWeSznOkHWiWdDhD97c10&news=true

Anon., *The Nativity,* Icon, c1475 (Gostinopolye Church of Saint Nicholas) Public Domain, Attribution: https://commons.wikimedia.org/wiki/File:Nativity_from_Gostinopolye_(c._1475,_Banco_Intesa).jpg

Jesus Teaching in the Temple, stained glass window, (University of King's College chapel, Halifax, Canada). Attribution: photo by Lokwing Wong.

Van Gogh, Vincent, *The Sower*, oil on canvas, 1888 (Kroller Muller

Gallery, Otterlo, Netherlands) 64,2x80,3 cm https://commons.wikimedia.org/wiki/File:Vincent_van_Gogh_-_The_Sower_-_c._17-28_June_1888.jpg

Munch, Edvard, *The Scream,* oil, tempera, pastels and crayon on cardboard 1893 91cmx73.5 cm, (National Gallery, Oslo, Norway) https://en.wikipedia.org/wiki/The_Scream#/media/File:Edvard_Munch,_1893,_The_Scream,_oil,_tempera_and_pastel_on_cardboard,_91_x_73_cm,_National_Gallery_of_Norway.jpg

Master of the Lehman Crucifixion, *Noli me Tangere,* fresco, active c. 1352-1399 (National Gallery) 542x800. Wikidata: https://www.wikidata.org/wiki/Q26692367

Anon. *The Good Shepherd,* mosaic, c. 400 (Mausoleum of Galla Placidia), photograph from Wikipedia, by Petar Milošević.

Saint Francis Master/Giotto, *Legend of Saint Francis #15 'Sermon to the Birds',* 1297-1300 (Basilica de San Francesco, Assisi). https://commons.wikimedia.org/wiki/Saint_Francis_cycle_in_the_Upper_Church_of_San_Francesco_at_Assisi#:~:text=The%20legend%20of%20Saint%20Francis,the%20walls%20of%20the%20transept.

Doré, Gustave, *Par, 31 Rosa celeste*, ink drawing in Alighieri, Dante. 1892. *The Divine Comedy*. trans. Henry Francis Cary ed., London, Paris & Melbourne: Cassell & Company (Retrieved on 13 July 2009).

Anon. Labyrinth pavement, early 13th century, Chartres Cathedral.
Photo: EinDao, 20 January, 2019.
https://commons.wikimedia.org/wiki/File:Labyrinth_der_Kathedrale_von_Notre-Dame_de_Chartres_in_Stein.jpg

IMAGES IN TEXT VOL II

Duccio di Buoninsegna, *Maestà,* 1308-1311, tempera and gold on wood 84in x 156in (Museo dell'Opera Metropolitana del Duomo, Siena), p.60.

Caravaggio, *The Calling of Saint Matthew*, 1599-1600, oil (San Luigi del Francesi, Rome), p.93.

Brueghel, *The Conversion of Saul,* 1657, oil on panel 43in x 63in (Kunsthistorisches Museum, Vienna).

Pisano, Giovanni, *Cardinal Virtues supported by Faith, Hope and Charity,* 12th-13th c., Holy Water Font Fuorcivitas, Image: By I, Sailko, CC BY-SA 3.0, https://commons.wikimedia.org/w/index.php?curid=14880113
San Giovanni Fuorcivitas, interno, acquasantiera delle virtù, p.242,

Doré, Gustave, *Par, 31 Rosa celeste*, ink drawing in Alighieri, Dante. 1892. *The Divine Comedy*. trans. Henry Francis Cary ed., London, Paris & Melbourne: Cassell & Company (Retrieved on 13 July 2009), p. 271.